# Everyday SEL in Elementary School

With this new book from educational consultant Carla Tantillo Philibert, you'll gain practical strategies for teaching Social-Emotional Learning (SEL), mindfulness, and movement to help your elementary students maintain positive relationships, assume responsibility, become bodily aware, and grow into productive, contributing citizens. You'll find out how to lead students through games, simple yoga poses, breathing techniques, and other activities that are easy to incorporate and help you manage your classroom. Topics include:

- Empowering your students to understand their emotions, improve their focus, manage stress, and regulate their behavior through structured activities
- Introducing your students to the concept of SEL and setting up your own SEL classroom
- Engaging your students in activities to strengthen peer-to-peer communication, community-building, and leadership skills
- Allowing your students to test their SEL skills through interactive stories and class discussions
- Honing your own SEL competency through professional development sessions so your students can get the most out of their SEL experience

The book also offers a Professional Development Facilitator's Guide to help you and your colleagues master the core concepts of SEL and implement them effectively in the classroom. The appendix provides additional strategies for overcoming common difficulties when first beginning your school's SEL journey.

**Carla Tantillo Philibert** is the founder of Mindful Practices, one of Chicago's leading school wellness organizations, and oversees a team of 25 dedicated practitioners who empower teachers and students across the nation with wellness and Social-Emotional Learning strategies to create a more effective educational environment.

## Other Eye On Education Books, available from Routledge

(www.routledge.com/eyeoneducation)

# Everyday SEL in Elementary School

## Integrating Social-Emotional Learning and Mindfulness Into Your Classroom

Carla Tantillo Philibert

Routledge
Taylor & Francis Group

NEW YORK AND LONDON

First published 2016
by Routledge
711 Third Avenue, New York, NY 10017

and by Routledge
2 Park Square, Milton Park, Abingdon, Oxon OX14 4RN

*Routledge is an imprint of the Taylor & Francis Group, an informa business*

*Library of Congress Cataloging in Publication Data*
Names: Tantillo Philibert, Carla, author.
Title: Everyday SEL in elementary school : integrating social-emotional learning and mindfulness into your classroom / by Carla Tantillo Philibert.
Description: New York : Routledge, 2016. | Includes bibliographical references.
Identifiers: LCCN 2015047213 | ISBN 9781138903142 (hardback) | ISBN 9781138903159 (pbk.) | ISBN 9781315697079 (e-book)
Subjects: LCSH: Affective education. | Social learning. | Mindfulness (Psychology) | Social values–Study and teaching (Elementary) | Social skills–Study and teaching (Elementary)
Classification: LCC LB1072 .T36 2016 | DDC 370.15/34–dc23
LC record available at http://lccn.loc.gov/2015047213

ISBN: 978-1-138-90314-2 (hbk)
ISBN: 978-1-138-90315-9 (pbk)
ISBN: 978-1-315-69707-9 (ebk)

Typeset in Palatino
by Wearset Ltd, Boldon, Tyne and Wear

For Rob, my loving muse, patient husband, and supportive thought partner

# Contents

# Meet the Author

**Carla Tantillo Philibert** founded the Mindful Practices team in 2006; the organization offers innovative Social-Emotional Learning (SEL), yoga, and wellness programs to over 150 schools across the country. A certified yoga teacher with a master's degree in curriculum and instruction, Carla was a founding teacher and curriculum director of a high-poverty school in Chicago. She has taught at both the secondary and elementary levels, is the co-creator of Hip-HopYoga™, and is a highly qualified professional development provider. Carla is also the author of *Cooling Down Your Classroom: Using Yoga, Relaxation and Breathing Strategies to Help Students Learn to Keep Their Cool* (2012). Carla and her husband Rob happily welcomed a daughter to their family in May of 2015 and enjoy long adventure walks with Little D. and their collie around downtown Chicago.

# Acknowledgments

There are so many patient, kind, and compassionate folks who are part of this book's journey. As a brand-new mother, I relied on many loving caregivers to step in to take Little D. for a walk, sing a song, or share a book, to buy me just a few more hours to write each day. Auntie Cathy, Precious, Ruby, Stefanie, Nana, and my dear father, Pat, your time and patience are truly appreciated. I am indebted to Erika Panichelli, the dynamic and hard-working Program Coordinator of our Mindful Practices team. Erika worked many, many long nights to make sure the team was nurtured and growing. Our Mindful Practices family has been indispensable in sharing their wisdom, ideas, and feedback for the activities included within. I am humbled every day by the experience of leading such a hard-working, dedicated, and innovative team. Additionally, I would like to thank Chicago Public Schools, Chicago International Charter Schools, and our many fabulous school partners across the country for opening your doors and sharing your amazing school communities with us. You have truly given us a home to take risks and learn together.

I particularly thank my mother, Violet, who gave me the strength to write my first book. She encouraged me – made me believe I could do it – and then helped me assemble it in her basement with the help of our dear friend Mary, and a plastic comb binding machine. Mom and Dad, I am forever in your debt for all you have done for me and Mindful Practices.

I am swimming in gratitude to my warm, thoughtful, and encouraging editor, Lauren Davis, her assistant, Marlena Sullivan, our copy-editor, Lucy Metzger, project manager Emma Critchley, and the supportive Routledge family. I am honored to write for such an innovative, fresh, and mindful team.

Most of all I thank my loving husband, Rob. As the sleep-deprived father of a newborn, he selflessly cared for our daughter on weekends so that I could relax into the writing process. His encouragement, creative input, and patience with my "This is the final draft, I promise!" speech gave me the space to reflect and grow as a writer, mother, and partner. Rob, you are the love of my life. Your positive impact knows no bounds.

# Introduction

After academics, what is the purpose of anything we devote time to in our busy classrooms? To help students grow into people that have positive relationships, are gainfully employed, and are good folks who volunteer at animal shelters on Sundays or help elderly ladies with their groceries. Isn't it that simple? If so, then devoting valuable classroom time to Social-Emotional Learning (SEL) and mindfulness is a way to empower our students with the life-long learning tools that will serve them long into adulthood, such as being present, responsible, bodily aware, and collaborative.

When I work with schools across the country to develop sustainable SEL and mindfulness programs, I often kick off our initial professional development session with a question such as:

> If you were to bump into a former student at the grocery store, would you rather she remembered the details of the academic content you delivered ("My two favorite elements were Strontium and Scandium because …") or that she had the social and emotional skills to be a productive, present, compassionate citizen of the world? Would you be more impressed if she could remember the protagonist's name in *To Kill a Mockingbird* or if she was excelling at a career because she learned, among other things, how to manage her emotions and engage in healthy peer-to-peer communication?

When asked, almost all teachers respond that they want their former students to be positive, present, and contributing citizens in the world. However, in the next breath I sometimes hear an educator say, "Well. Um … I'm a science teacher. I didn't sign up to teach this touchy-feely stuff. It is not my job. Students should be learning this stuff at home." And, of course, we all agree. Yes, our students *should* be learning social and emotional skills at home, but in some homes they are not. And if they don't learn them at all, then they will never get a chance to use all that awesome science they learned, because they won't have the requisite social skills to hold down a job. Unfortunately, we all know that Ohm's Law is not needed to sit on the couch and play video games.

Now, this is a false comparison on some level, because as educators we don't want one or the other, we want both. We want our students to remember the protagonist's name and have the social and emotional skills to excel in life. To help them do so, we need to prioritize SEL content and methodology in our classrooms and view a student's ability to deal successfully with life's stresses as the standardized test for SEL.

The million-dollar question then becomes: how do you convert the disbelievers so that SEL, mindfulness, and yoga/movement – together what I call Mindful Practices – can be built into the school's culture authentically across disciplines? This can be a challenge, as SEL or mindfulness often can be seen as a separate add-on that requires little or no integration or proficiency on the part of the practitioner. Without integration or practitioner competency, the benefits of SEL can be limited and short term, at best. SEL, mindfulness, and yoga/movement are best implemented when they are integrated into the climate and culture not just of the classroom but of the school, so that there is a model for the students to reference. With the help of this book, you can be that model, enjoy a positive climate and culture, simplify your classroom management, and provide your students with the social and emotional strategies they need to be successful in and outside of the classroom.

When I finished my teaching certification in 2000, I left school having seen the term "Social-Emotional Learning" included on only one professor's syllabus. Mindfulness was absent all together. Many of the teachers I coach (from urban Chicago to hilly New Hampshire to rural Oklahoma) had a similar pre-service experience. In contrast, in 2015 almost all 50 states have early childhood standards for SEL, with four states having adopted K–12 standards (a number that will hopefully double by the time this book goes to print). Mindfulness has had a somewhat different trajectory, but with the inclusion of yoga in schools gaining popularity, mindfulness is a close second, as the two practices are interlinked in many ways.

So, while the movement to include SEL and mindfulness in schools gains momentum, as educators we find ourselves in a difficult spot. We are adopting state standards for Social-Emotional Learning content that many of our teachers are not competent to deliver due to a lack of training. To complicate the matter, they may be unaware of the gaps in their efficacy or lack the motivation to learn and share the content of their learning.

The classical paradigm of teacher-disciplines-student, student-corrects-behavior-because-teacher-said-so may seem to provide a well-managed classroom, but at what cost? Instead of creating present, compassionate, and empowered learners, it builds reliance on the classroom manager and their directives. Students aren't asked to learn how to be self-aware or self-regulate, they are simply asked to comply. In turn, students regulate their behavior in the short term, but we often see a resurgence of that behavior in a different classroom the following year. Compliance may provide a school with great test scores and discipline rates while students are within their highly structured environment, but later achievement numbers for these same students (such as high school graduation rates) are often lackluster once learners exit the schoolhouse doors.

When working with teachers across the country, I often hear the question, "Why was Javier so well behaved for Ms. Munoz last year and is such a terror in my class this year?" I refer to this trend as "teacher magic": when a teacher intuitively adapts her instruction to meet the needs of a child, but the strategies were never explicitly taught and the student ends the year without an improved sense of self-awareness. Often these students leave school without the words to express what positively or negatively impacts their learning or an awareness of how they learn best.

The Mindful Practices SEL competencies that are highlighted in this book – Self-Awareness, Self-Regulation, Social Awareness, and the balance between Self-Efficacy and Social Harmony – are skills we assume our teachers possess simply by virtue of being nurturers and educators. And many teachers do. These skills are often intuitive, as the good educators naturally "get" kids. They understand what students need and shift the energy of their classroom accordingly. However, some of the best teachers I have observed, when asked, cannot put this practice into words. While these teachers are effective classroom managers, without the words to explain their methodology, students may excel in their class and struggle in the next. The techniques in this book will provide teachers and students the tools to find their voices and put their practices into words.

## Where Do We Begin?

We begin with developing teacher competency and understanding around how this content influences the climate and culture of their classrooms and, in turn, student achievement. If we expect teachers to implement state SEL standards with fidelity or Mindful Practices in their classrooms, then we must abandon kits or programs that work as a quick fix and find time for building competency with quality professional development. Having teachers simply read a scripted activity or switch on some technology is not enough. We must move away from these practices as a Band-Aid® or something we do once a week just to "meet our SEL minutes" and look at these as life-long learning tools for both teachers and students. Sure, buying a quick kit with scripted material seems much easier. But, if you are looking for easy, then you are in the wrong profession. Teaching, working with kids, is high-stakes. Doing something the right way, the way that we know has the greatest positive impact on student learning, is our professional responsibility.

Before diving into the Mindful Practices approach outlined in this book, it must be said that it is incomplete. For this work to have the greatest impact, we need to pair teachers with fields outside of education. We need to connect with pediatricians, trauma therapists, nutritionists, cultural experts, physical therapists – people who can help us, as educators, better understand the body's psychosomatic response to stress and how it impacts learning along with information that can make the material more culturally sensitive and responsive to the populations we are serving. These fields also have quantitative practices to help monitor the work's impact on students. While there are some progress-monitoring SEL tools or games available for iPads or computers, technology is often, by design, a solitary pursuit for the students and so the SOCIAL component of Social-Emotional Learning is often merely theoretical. I have found that SEL programs which rely solely on students hearing or reading a social scenario and anticipating the appropriate response is not a substitute for students experientially walking through the Social Awareness strategies in real time. It is one thing to read or imagine a response to a potential problem, and another to experience the frustration and anxiety about resolving the conflict and then *still* engage in effective peer-to-peer communication and team building.

I present this Mindful Practices model to you as a humble how-to guide for creating an impactful SEL school experience. I designed these tools to help educators and school leaders implement sustainable SEL, mindfulness, and yoga/movement programming, or what we call Mindful Practices, with fidelity, and encourage you to reach out to other professions, outside of education, to widen the scope of practice even further.

Given the emphasis on school climate, culture, and building teacher competency, this approach necessitates that educators leave their comfort zones. This is not a student-centered program with a singular focus of merely knocking SEL off a school's to-do list. Instead it's an integrated approach that calls on the school stakeholders to Be the Solution by being active, present, and reflective.

The path outlined inside this book borrows ideas from some of the most thoughtful and innovative work in the field: mindfulness, yoga, cognitive behavioral therapy (CBT), trauma research, Peter Senge on systems thinking in schools, Brene Brown on vulnerability, Gretchen Rubin on happiness, Ronald D. Siegel on mindfulness, Charlotte Danielson's teaching framework (most notably Domain 2), Doug Lemov's classroom management strategies, Harry Wong's warm, organized classroom, and best practices gleaned from John Hattie's work relating to achievement. I also give a proud nod to my own Mindful Practices team, who helped me design, implement, tweak, test, implement again, refine – and then redesign some of the activities contained in this book: thoughtful activities such as Stefanie Piatkiewicz's fabulous Brain Massage, Ericka Lashley's fun Movement-Based SEL Definition, Vienna Webb's relaxing breathing activities, Precious Jennings' wise inclusion of cues to center the body in the Warm-Up Activities, or Lara Veon's mindful addition of trauma-sensitive language in the SEL Scenarios. My Auntie Cathy helped me develop the early childhood modifications and included thoughtful adaptations for students with exceptionalities. My fantastic mother Violet, a former principal who was one of the first to adopt our yoga-based SEL program at her school along with Mary Kusper, her right hand, and our dynamic Program Coordinator, Erika Panichelli, have also spent hours helping me mold and shape our professional development programming so that it is meaningful and relevant for teachers. Many of the programs out there conveniently focus on either the "SELF" or the "SOCIAL " component of SEL, for the ease of implementation. I am proud that our Mindful Practices approach addresses the school experience as a balance of SELF and SOCIAL for both the student and the teacher. As the Founder, I am proud of the work that Mindful Practices does, because it has been developed over a ten-year period in response to both student and teacher needs. My team has worked in demographically and socio-economically diverse settings to develop these activities. We have been testing these SEL and wellness strategies in the field, as boots on the ground, since 2006.

I hope you will find my Mindful Practices model both helpful and practical. Besides its innovative fusion of SEL and mindfulness, the prioritization of physical movement is one more component that makes this approach unique. I created these strategies to help develop your SEL competency and that of your students, along with practical implementation tools for the school and classroom. I encourage you to envision how each of the ideas can be modified to your specific classroom. Utilize these strategies to build a sustainable SEL program for your classroom, but, more importantly, take time to customize the approach so it is relevant and meaningful for you and your students.

As you dive into the book, please don't hesitate to contact me with questions. I love hearing from teachers, administrators, parents, counselors, and school stakeholders! You can reach me at Carla@MindfulPracticesYoga.com or through my website at www.MindfulPracticesYoga.com.

As we move forward on this journey together, I cue you to pause and take a breath. Even though we are the adults in our classrooms, we are not perfect. Moreover, we do not need to be. We simply need to accept ourselves in the present and try our best to model Mindful Practices for our students each day. The school experience is the balance of SELF and SOCIAL, which includes our calm days and our triggered days. It is our job to teach our students the life skill of coping with stress and anxiety as much as it is our job to make sure they know a quadratic equation or the structure of a haiku poem. As I say in the explanation of the Ready to Learn Breath (p. 78), it is important that we "give ourselves permission not to be perfect. The most important thing is that we try our best."

# 1

# Defining Social-Emotional Learning for Students and Teachers

When I taught high school there was a student of mine, Roger, who couldn't concentrate on my oh-so-fabulous poetry lesson because his basic needs were not meet. I didn't see that. I saw a student that was disrupting my lesson by fidgeting and talking to the students next to him. I strongly disciplined him, as I did the next day *and* the day after that when the behavior continued. Sharing his behavior that week with my colleagues over lunch (admittedly in a less-than-compassionate "I don't know what is wrong with Roger this week" type way), I discovered that his younger sister, Brandy, had been reprimanded for sneaking food out of the school cafeteria. Putting all the pieces together, we figured out that Roger was hungry. His younger siblings were hungry. His mom, who had a problem with heroin and had gone on "benders" before, had deserted them and Roger didn't know where she was or where their next meal was coming from. Of course, my fabulous poetry lesson didn't matter to him! He was stuck in the panic of meeting the basic needs for himself and his siblings with zero resources or support. This was coupled with concern for his mother's well-being along with hiding the truth from the school and his siblings so that they would not end up in foster care, again. Examining the climate and culture of my classroom at the time, I found that there was no mechanism for him to meet his emotional or physical needs. I naively thought that my dynamic lesson was enough to engage him in learning, regardless of what was happening outside of the schoolhouse doors.

For teachers to be effective, students must feel comfortable stepping into vulnerability. The classroom environment must honor students' physical, mental, and emotional needs without judgment, so that they can move out of "survival mode" (fight, flight, or freeze) and be Ready to Learn. Given the politics and legal restrictions of schools, a situation like Roger's is complex on many levels. But, at the end of the day, the lesson is a good one. If our students' basic needs are not met, they cannot be present and Ready to Learn. Practicing SEL, mindfulness, or yoga could not have put food in Roger's stomach, but it could have helped him deal with the crippling anxiety of the unknown.

This book fuses the traditional practices of Social-Emotional Learning (SEL), mindfulness, yoga, and physical movement into one comprehensive approach we call Mindful Practices (see Figure 1.1). Mindful Practices are those practices that help cultivate awareness of body and mind in both personal and interpersonal situations so that one can operate with compassion for self and others. While SEL or mindfulness on their own do not traditionally include yoga, movement, or student wellness, Mindful Practices looks at the needs of the whole child: emotional, physical, and mental; when these three are in balance, a student is able to be present and Ready to Learn. Mindfulness is an important part of these practices as its inclusion into the classroom setting creates "present learners," or students and teachers that are empowered to move through activation so they are able to focus on the task at hand.

The Mindful Practices approach moves beyond a program that teachers merely implement, into a method of crafting a classroom that meets the competing needs of the whole child. Looking at everything from a student's overall wellness (Is lack of sleep keeping a student from being present? Is a student's physical need to move his body keeping him from being able to focus?) to what drives student interactions (Is there a conflict with a peer that keeps a student's mind focused on "survival" instead of being present in the classroom?), and, most importantly, how does the energy of the classroom need to shift so that the students are present, focused, and Ready to Learn? When we frame the implementation of Mindful Practices around creating a classroom of students that are present and Ready to Learn, we are empowered to address the roadblocks that often keep us from teaching to our full potential.

This book provides the tools needed for a successful program implementation, namely the creation of a classroom climate and culture that bring practitioner and student into a compassionate and safe connection. We'll explore the tenet that the goals of SEL, such as the ability to handle stress effectively and the ability to regulate emotions, are commonalities shared across class, gender, and culture for both educator and student.

**Figure 1.1** Social-Emotional Learning, mindfulness and movement in the classroom: Mindful Practices' two-part transformative process

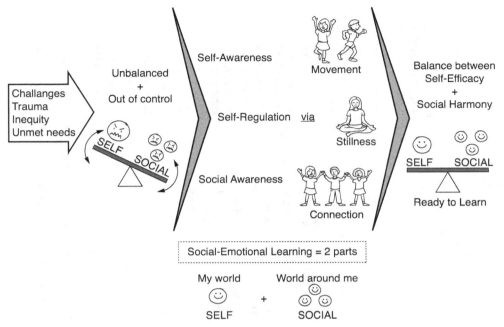

The Mindful Practices model outlined in this book moves teachers from viewing these practices as something that "underperforming children" need as a "special treatment" to understanding them as a collective learning process needed by all, because everyone regularly experiences stress, anxiety, and negativity. When the situation is reframed from the adult and child being in opposition to the collective working towards a common, interpersonal goal, not only are life-long skills developed, but the classroom climate and culture improve as well.

These Mindful Practices provide teachers and students with the tools to understand how their world works, their connection to it, how they express themselves within in it, and how they can balance their own needs alongside the needs of the collective. Again, the emphasis shifts from a handful of "problem children" receiving the service to SEL being a "Tier 1" intervention for the entire class. The Mindful Practices model outlined in this book empowers teachers and students with a framework to cultivate Self-Awareness, Self-Regulation, and Social Awareness through intentional practice in a safe and structured classroom environment so that the balance can be found between Self-Efficacy and Social Harmony (Figure 1.2).

**Figure 1.2** The Mindful Practices' model

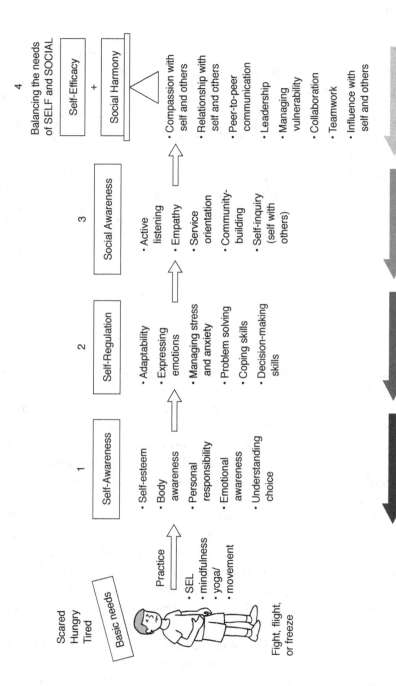

Quite simply, the Mindful Practices approach utilizes mindfulness, yoga, team building, breath work, and and movement strategies to teach the following four SEL competencies:

1. **Self-Awareness:** self-esteem, body awareness, personal responsibility, emotional awareness, and understanding choice. Practicing these activities and cultivating an understanding of SELF moves the learner from powerlessness to empowered.

2. **Self-Regulation:** adaptability, expressing emotions, managing stress/anxiety, problem solving, coping skills, self-inquiry and decision-making skills. Practicing these activities and learning how to Self-Regulate moves the learner from impulsivity to positively navigating behavioral choices.

3. **Social Awareness:** active listening, empathy, service orientation, and community-building. Practicing these skills and cultivating Social Awareness moves learners from a reactive, victimized mindset to a more proactive, communal view of the world around them. (See Table A.1 for sample of explicit teaching.)

4. **Balance between Self-Efficacy and Social Harmony:** leadership, managing vulnerability, collaboration, teamwork, influence of SELF and others, understanding relationships with SELF and others, operating with compassion towards SELF and others, and peer-to-peer communication. When practiced and in balance, learners feel centered, present, and like a valued and contributing member of the world around them. This competency also reflects the individual's ability to find her voice and balance the needs of the SELF with the needs of the SOCIAL, without projection, assumption, or excessive self-sacrifice.

Display these four SEL competencies close to your POP Chart and SEL word wall (see p. 36). For SEL programming to be impactful, it must have a consistent presence in students' lives. (To build competency, SEL terminology is shown in bold in lessons and stories.)

While there are many definitions or models of Social-Emotional Learning out there, by fusing SEL, mindfulness, and yoga/physical movement, the Mindful Practices model includes a focus on student wellness that often goes unaddressed in other programs. Our model prioritizes the

**Table 1.1** Rubric to monitor the school's progress in SEL practice

School name:                                                    Academic year:

Committee members:

| Stages | Descriptors | Timeline |
|--------|-------------|----------|
| **5. Sustainable** | **On-going implementation assessment: Have we created a sustainable model?**<br>◆ POP Chart and Call to Action are visible in and messaged around school. SEL is practiced daily in the classrooms and included in the morning announcements.<br>◆ School SEL + Wellness initiatives are sustainable and meet the needs of school stakeholders, such as students, parents, teachers, staff, and community members. Self-care is prioritized.<br>◆ SEL Team leads PD and Teacher Institutes that reinforce SEL practices. Climate and culture expectations of both classroom and school are clearly defined. Consistent SEL messaging and common language across school by all stakeholders and adults in students' lives.<br>◆ Communication tools such as the Agreements, Boom Board! and Pants on Fire! are utilized across disciplines by all school stakeholders.<br>◆ Grade bands meet regularly to plan and implement end-of-year SEL Service Learning Project. Methods are developed to connect SEL practices to home and community. | **School year ends** |
| **4. Experienced** | **On-going implementation assessment: How have we grown?**<br>◆ SEL and parent Wellness Nights are thriving and gain momentum within the community. SEL is embedded in school sports and extracurricular activities.<br>◆ School SEL initiatives reflect communication between SEL Team, PE teachers, wellness stakeholders (social worker, nurse, etc.), parents, and school faculty/staff.<br>◆ SEL and teacher self-care are practiced during PD and Teacher Institute days. PE teachers and wellness stakeholders receive supplemental training. School climate/cultural pieces reflect whole-school SEL + Wellness messaging.<br>◆ Grade bands meet to develop consistent classroom SEL practices and to begin planning SEL Service Learning Project for the school community. | **8 months** |

| 3. Capable | **Assessment of skills learned: Where are we and what do we need to improve?** | **5 months** |
|---|---|---|
| | ◆ School SEL and wellness initiatives show thoughtful placement and are reflective of needs of parents, students, and community. Call to Action messaging becomes more common among school stakeholders. | |
| | ◆ SEL and teacher self-care are modeled and reinforced during PD and Teacher Institute days. PE teachers, wellness stakeholders (social worker, nurse, etc.) and classroom teachers receive supplemental training. | |
| | ◆ SEL Team meets quarterly. | |
| | ◆ POP Chart visible in most classrooms. Wellness/physical activity is practiced 2–3 times a week in the classrooms. | |
| | ◆ Impact of SEL and wellness initiative on school climate and culture becomes tangible. Teacher self-care is promoted and incentivized monthly. | |
| 2. Emerging | **Reviewing and refining practices and expectations** | **2 months** |
| | ◆ School SEL and wellness initiatives, including teacher self-care, emerge and begin to balance priorities. POP Chart visible in some classrooms. Wellness/physical activity is practiced occasionally (1–2 times a week) in the classrooms. | |
| | ◆ SEL Team is created. A Call to Action, such as "Be the Solution," "In the Zone," or "Ready to Learn," is adopted. | |
| | ◆ Communication emerges between PE teachers, wellness stakeholders (social worker, nurse, etc.), and classroom teachers. SEL theme in morning announcements. | |
| | ◆ SEL emerges as a theme in both faculty PD and school climate and culture. | |
| | ◆ Parents are surveyed regarding interest in community SEL and Wellness Nights. | |
| 1. Baseline | **Establishing baseline, practices, and expectations** | **School year begins** |
| | ◆ SEL and wellness are not practiced at school level. Palpable division between teachers and other school staff (i.e. bus drivers, cafeteria staff, building engineers, etc.). | |
| | ◆ No communication between PE teachers, wellness stakeholders (social worker, nurse, etc.), and classroom teachers. No SEL theme in morning announcements. | |
| | ◆ If present, SEL and wellness initiatives are random, inconsistent, and unbalanced. No common language. No consistent SEL messaging. | |
| | ◆ Relaxation/physical activity is not practiced daily in classrooms. | |
| | ◆ School/classroom climate and culture is nebulous or undefined. No "Call to Action." | |

connection between a student's health and wellness and their ability to be a present, focused, and collaborative member of the classroom community. "I only had a bag of Skittles for breakfast and I am having a difficult time concentrating on my reading quiz." Or, "I know I am anxious about playing with those older girls at recess again because my palms are sweating and my stomach hurts." This innovative approach helps address the needs of the whole child by creating the space to learn the lessons of the body through awareness of psychosomatic cues and their connection to students' mental and emotional state.

Our model places Self-Awareness as the necessary precursor to Self-Regulation, with the journey of the SELF progressing from basic needs through to SOCIAL harmony. The emphasis here is on the personal and interpersonal, as school and life necessitate that learners balance the needs of the personal ("I want to get an A on this spelling test!") with the demands of the interpersonal ("But I can't concentrate because the student next to me keeps talking, who I want to punch, but know I can't!"). School is a personal pursuit housed within a social construct. To be an effective student, learners must astutely juggle both sets of priorities. We should not assume that students have the necessary skillset for this; consistently practicing SEL and mindfulness provides students with these tools.

The Mindful Practices SEL competencies are linear, with material that must be scaffolded and tracked, the same way we would scaffold and track traditional academic content. Just as a student must learn to add before he can subtract, we can't expect a student to regulate a behavior if he is unaware of it. In fact, the balance between Self-Efficacy and Social Harmony (the duality between the personal and the interpersonal) is achieved when teachers and students build competency by working through the stages of Self-Awareness, Self-Regulation, and Social Awareness.

Our definition is also written so that it can apply to learners of all ages, including adults. This is intentional, because the SEL competency we have as teachers is more important than the competency of our students. As the teachers, we are the delivery vehicle by which the information is conveyed. Our SEL proficiency cannot be assumed simply because we teach, the same way we wouldn't assume that all teachers in the USA are proficient in teaching Language Arts simply because they live in an English-speaking country.

In many schools I have worked with across the country, stakeholders are utilizing effective SEL tools across the building, but no common language has been developed and nothing has been codified. While there may be wonderful SEL practices taking place, there is no common language in the school around the work and students spend the bulk of their time engaging in a form of SEL code-switching from room to room, instead of being present in their practice. SEL may be called "SEL" in a student's classroom and then "Cool Down" when they go to see the dean, a "Wellness Break" when they get to their PE class and then "Relaxation Time" when they are working with the social worker. While each of these educators is well intentioned and, most likely, implementing solid practices, the students spend their time decoding what is happening in which setting, instead of learning from the practices themselves.

To model how to move forward with intentionality and consistency for all school stakeholders, my **eight recommendations** are listed below.

## 1. Teach with Intention: Treat SEL Like Academic Content

SEL, mindfulness, and yoga or physical movement need to be taught with the same intentionality as core content areas. One would never teach long division or nouns as an isolated concept, and this same thinking should be applied to SEL. The concept of empathy cannot be taught in a week, unrelated to other SEL competencies. Instead, the material must be scaffolded (as shown in Figure 1.2), taught and retaught when mastery is not achieved.

Social-Emotional Learning is, by its very nature, social. This material cannot be taught solely using technology, worksheets, or scripted material. The balance of SELF and SOCIAL is required for the delivery of the content to have an impact. Delivery must take place over time, as Catherine Cook-Cottone's work around dosage suggests. John Hattie's work in *Visible Learning* notes that providing "social skill training on a regular and sustained basis" and found that this was most effective "when interventions lasted for 40 lessons or more." Keeping these recommendations in mind, our Mindful Practices program starts each day with a five-minute POP Chart Check-In to empower the students to Pause (breathe), Own (their emotions/feelings), and Practice (a solution) (a sample chart is shown in Figure 2.4). Formal SEL instruction begins each week with a culturally relevant SEL Story on Mondays, and either a SELF (personal) or SOCIAL (interpersonal) activity on Tuesday to Friday, depending on the needs of the class as identified by the teacher. We have found that 25 minutes is the perfect time frame for an SEL lesson. However, given that time is often scarce in our current high-stakes testing environment, this book contains lessons that average between 10 and 25 minutes in duration. The time spent on these Mindful Practices will pay for itself throughout the school day.

Your Classroom SEL practice every Monday:

1. Morning POP Chart Check-In
2. A Social-Emotional Learning Story

Your Classroom SEL practice, Tuesday–Friday:

1. Morning POP Chart Check-In
2. A SELF or SOCIAL activity

Additionally, the POP Chart activities are there at any time if you need your class to Get In the Zone, or if individual students need a break to relax, energize, or focus.

When the new activity is learned, a card for that activity is added to the POP Chart. That way, the activity can be practiced again throughout the week, during both the morning check-in (if a student identifies a need for herself), or throughout the day (if the teacher identifies a need for the group). To implement with fidelity, the recommended dosage or intervention is 10–25 minutes per day, including the Morning POP Chart Check-In.

## 2. Fix the Problem of Practice: Develop Teacher Competency

Educators cannot teach what they cannot model. If we adopted violin standards at the state level requiring each and every classroom teacher to deliver proficient violin instruction, there would be, rightfully, an outrage among educators. Administrators across the country would decry that we have not trained our teachers to deliver violin instruction appropriately. They would fear that lack of teacher knowledge would lead to unsatisfactory teaching and the spreading of misinformation about the content. There would be concern that suggesting that anyone can teach violin without proper training would devalue the content and its delivery. And all these concerns would undoubtedly be valid.

This begs the question: if we would never think to adopt violin standards in this way, why did we do it with SEL and are we sacrificing the fidelity of the practice in the process? We must move schools beyond simply adopting the state SEL standards or a mindfulness program. We agree that we would never just hand a teacher a violin and expect him to be able to teach it proficiently. SEL must be viewed the same way if we expect to impact the climate and culture of the classrooms in which the learning is taking place.

All that being said, state standards for SEL are a *big* step in the right direction as they move Social-Emotional Learning from the realm of suggested and easily dismissed content to a core competency vital to a student's academic success. (And I applaud policy makers for the countless hours they have spent advocating for this work!) The important next step is to look at the implementation side of standards. How can we develop our competency as teachers at a rate that meets the need for quality implementation?

I have found that the teachers who are most successful implementing these practices are those that find their voice with the work. Educators who can embrace the duality between teacher and learner view the experiential learning process as the reflective springboard for effectively teaching SEL. If you are reading this book on a school-wide level, you might find the chapter on impactful professional development (Chapter 9) to be helpful. It shows how you and your colleagues can work together not on just speaking the language of the content, but on modeling it daily to shift the climate and culture of your school building.

If you are an innovative teacher who is reading this book alone, Bravo! You are the agent of change at your school. One breath at a time, you and your students will begin to witness positive changes of your classroom. By cultivating Self-Awareness, you and your students will be empowered to Self-Regulate and reflect on how your experiences contribute to the collective classroom community. While this, in and of itself, is great, your colleagues will slowly begin to witness the changes as well.

> "Hey Alice, did you notice how Butch's students are much better behaved this semester? I wonder what he is doing differently?"

Slowly a buzz will begin to circulate, and it is at this point that I encourage you to lead a little mini-lesson from the professional development section (Chapter 9) at your school's next faculty meeting. Follow that up by inviting colleagues to visit your classroom during their preparatory periods to witness you "in action."

## 3. "Be the Solution": Create a Motivational Call to Action

Often, when I am visiting a new school, I will see signs for "Lion Pride," "Warrior Pride," or "Whatever-the-school-mascot-happens-to-be Pride." I will walk the halls and hear teachers witnessing "Lion Pride" among the students. When I stop to ask a random student what Lion behavior looks like or what it means to be a Lincoln Lion, the students will often respond with a comment about the reward, not the observable behavior. "Being a Lincoln Lion means I get a coupon and I get to go to the school store to get a bag of Flaming Hots."

This is problematic. Yes, we could enter into the age-old debate in education over intrinsic versus extrinsic motivation in school, but I would argue the problem isn't with the Flaming Hots (although it must be said that incentivizing junk food at a school is an unhealthy practice). No, it is with the lack of clear messaging from the school site. What does the school stand for? It can't be a bag of Flaming Hots, right?

What does your school stand for, and how can a Call to Action, or an instruction that begets an immediate response, be developed to communicate that rallying cry to all stakeholders in the building? What does *your Call to Action* look, sound, and feel like at your school?

When I was finalizing this section of the book I was working in New Hampshire with one of my favorite schools, Conway Elementary. They have a truly fantastic principal, dedicated teachers, and stellar SEL happening in certain classrooms, but the need to extend the practices across grade levels and outside of the schoolhouse doors had not been met. So Principal Hastings and I worked hand in hand to develop a simple, no-nonsense Call to Action that would speak to his students, teachers, and school community: Being In the Zone. Given its use in sports, this phrasing was familiar and catchy enough that his school community could easily adopt it.

Being In the Zone translated to being ready – whether it was ready to take a math test, ready to Be the Solution and resolve a conflict, or ready for the big game after school, a state of readiness became the rallying cry.

The state of readiness, or being present in the moment, is the same end goal as practicing mindfulness. Cueing the students to "Be In the Zone" helps them cultivate the awareness needed to shut out internal and external clutter so that they can be present and ready for the task at hand.

A Call to Action frames every problem or issue the students encounter as an opportunity to positively move a situation forward or contribute to the classroom community. "Fernando, what do you need to do to Get In the Zone, stop distracting the students next to you and focus on your writing prompt?"

Be the Solution, Being In the Zone, or whatever Call to Action is implemented, should work in all settings: classroom, lunchroom, playground, on the bus, lining up in the morning, and should be spoken by all school stakeholders. "Lori Ann, are we Being the Solution right now by cutting Shanesha in line?"

The Call to Action becomes a phrase heard round the school, messaged by every adult. SEL is no longer a sidebar add-on. It is a phrase, a code, a vital organ of the school culture. If I were visiting your school, I would hear the assistant principal use the Call to Action with a student in his office, I would hear the third-grade teacher use it with a student she had a pulled to the side for a quick behavioral chat, I would hear the woman running the lunch program use it with a student who was throwing a carrot, I would hear the bus driver use it to praise a student who stayed in his seat, I would hear the parent coordinator use it to praise a group of disgruntled parents at the PTA meeting, I would hear a parent saying it to their child as they dropped them off, I would hear the principal use it with her teachers at the faculty meeting. It rings throughout the school. It shifts the focus from being stuck in the problem to finding a solution and, most importantly, owning how that solution impacts both the personal and interpersonal aspect of school for students, teachers, parents, and administrators (Figure 1.3).

Peter Senge's work around schools as systems reinforces that educators should take their thinking to the larger, whole-school scale. For instance, "What can we, as the educators and stakeholders of Nola Elementary School, communicate across and within the system to define it?"

If an SEL program at a school is going to have any weight, schools need to stand for something and, as Senge notes, that something needs to be indicative of the larger system in which the school is housed. To cultivate that magical balance between Self-Efficacy and Social Harmony, students must feel that their actions impact that system. "Good" and "Bad" behavior cannot simply be defined by the classroom the students happen to be in at that moment, or else our students spend their time decoding the teacher's quirks instead of learning to be accountable to the larger school community.

"In Ms. Divito's Art room I can't write in pen, or else she gets mad. But she is fine if we don't raise our hands when we want to talk. In Mrs. Dixon's after-school class I can write in pen, but I have to put a heading on the paper and raise my hand if I want to talk, or else she gets upset. In Mr. Burr's second-grade class, he takes points off if we don't have a heading on our papers, but we can write in whatever we want and he has us hold up two fingers if we have a question instead of raising our hand."

**Figure 1.3** Your school's successful SEL communication

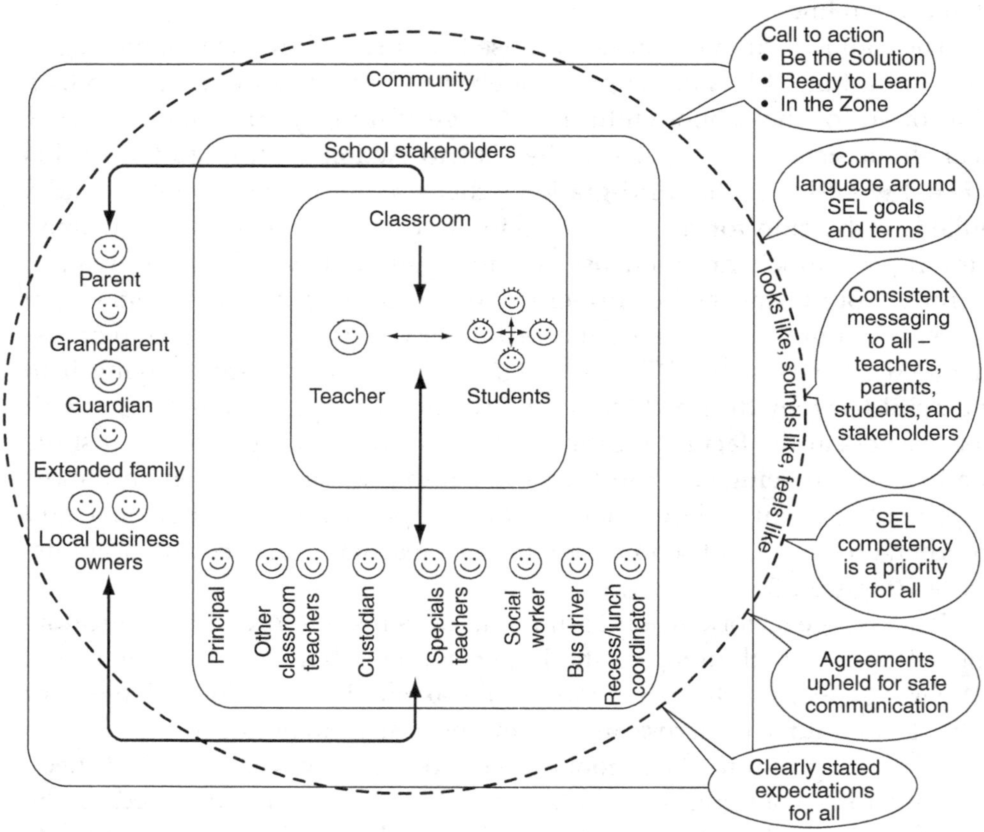

Community

School stakeholders

Classroom

Call to action
• Be the Solution
• Ready to Learn
• In the Zone

Common language around SEL goals and terms

Consistent messaging to all – teachers, parents, students, and stakeholders

SEL competency is a priority for all

Agreements upheld for safe communication

Clearly stated expectations for all

looks like, sounds like, feels like

Teacher    Students

Parent

Grandparent

Guardian

Extended family

Local business owners

Principal

Other classroom teachers

Custodian

Specials teachers

Social worker

Bus driver

Recess/lunch coordinator

Yes, we expect our students to keep track of all this and to be able to regulate their behavior, communicate with peers, and be present and Ready to Learn as well! It is no wonder when I ask students what Lion Pride is, their minds go to the reward. The behavioral expectations are a jumbled, random mess with personal preference as the only seeming rationale. We want students to be able to demonstrate the values of the Call to Action – to show that they know why they are here, what is expected of them, why it matters if they behave, and what we are all here to do – together. "Being a Lincoln Lion means that I am In the Zone, that I am focused, Ready to Learn and accountable to my school community."

Social-Emotional Learning and mindfulness instruction cannot be impactful if the canvas of the classroom is not clearly defined or emotionally and physically safe. Taking a cue from Charlotte Danielson's Domains and working towards "establishing an environment of respect and rapport (Domain 2)" by "Understanding your students (Domain 1)" is a terrific first step. By intentionally shifting the focus from "disciplining" students to creating self-reliant learners who are able to regulate their behavior, students are empowered to Be the Solution and Own their educational experience.

Awareness of this dual focus – on the SELF and the SOCIAL concurrently – is at the heart of the Mindful Practices approach. It cannot just be "empathy week" or SEL time on Wednesday morning and *that* is when students' minds are on Being In the Zone or Being the Solution. From the moment the principal opens the building the school experience is viewed, for all, through the Be the Solution lens. If someone is not Being the Solution – meaning she is stuck in a scarcity mindset, thinking only of problems and not of solutions – then Be The Solution is the rallying cry, the Call to Action, to shift her thinking back to what is best for the school or classroom community.

The first step for successful implementation is to build consensus on an appropriate Call to Action that is inclusive, meaningful, and culturally relevant for your school community. Develop common language and message it to teachers, parents, students, and community members. Give examples of what it is and what it is not. Provide school stakeholders with ample professional development so that they can not only help you develop it but also take ownership of it and implement it with fidelity. Include parents and auxiliary staff in the initiative, and remind them that they are, as adult presences in our students' lives, role models.

If you are an innovative teacher-leader who is beginning this program on her own, start by weaving the Call to Action into the fabric of your classroom. Consistently message it to your students as part of your classroom rules or expectations. Make it relevant and make it matter.

## 4. Educate the Whole Child: Healthy Body = Healthy Mind

There are multiple reasons to prioritize wellness in schools, but the first is that teachers need to be empowered to model healthy practices for students so that they can both meet their basic needs. If students are thirsty, we want them to reach for water, not soda or pop. If students are hungry, we want them to reach for almonds, not potato chips. We want students to make the connection between what they put into their bodies and how their bodies and minds function. Are they more Ready to Learn after a candy bar or a bag of baby carrots? How do sleeping, eating, drinking, stress, and exercise impact them as learners?

An additional layer to the wellness piece is being aware of our many students whose basic needs are not met. How do we, as educators who are with them eight hours a day, help them strategize positive solutions for being hungry or tired in our classrooms? When Terrice is falling asleep in class for the fifth day in a row, do we nudge him and say "Sleeping is for home, not for school" and simply leave it at that? When Amy is sneaking sunflower seeds out of her pocket during our math lesson because she is starving, do we simply give her a firm "put it away" look or do we check in with her after class to investigate the trend? As I outline on pages 9 and 10, students' ability to cultivate Self-Awareness and Self-Regulation is compromised when they are stuck in the panic of meeting their basic needs. As adults, we are the same way; we just have more resources to counter the anxiety of our basic needs not being met. If we had a restless night's sleep, we just swing by the faculty lounge for a cup of coffee. What if there is no coffee? What if there is no option to swing by the faculty lounge? Many of our students live in poverty where being hungry, tired, or perhaps not having clean shirts or socks is a daily reality. Their resources are limited and so school becomes the place that not only helps fill the gaps, but models healthy lifestyle choices that our students may not have access to at home.

This topic is a sensitive one and I have often heard teachers say, "Geez, really!? I have to worry about teaching these kids adverbs *and* worry about whether or not they have had breakfast or more than three hours' sleep? Isn't this basic needs stuff the parents' job?" Yes. It is the parents' job. But if the students are not learning the skills to manage these needs at home, how will they be able to counter the negative impact on their learning?

As educators, it is important that we do everything we can to model healthy practices throughout the school day, especially for students who are making very adult decisions when dealing with life outside the classroom. Some of our students are given money to buy their own breakfast at the corner store before school. This decision requires that students understand that sugar, caffeine, and nutritionally void foods negatively impact their learning. As parents are often not able to do this, for myriad reasons, the best way to communicate healthy lifestyle choices – what to eat, what to drink, methods of exercise, ways to deal with stress – is through appropriate teacher modeling. As America is topping the charts as one of the most obese countries in the world, often asking teachers to model healthy choices can be a delicate topic as teachers may be struggling with defining health and wellness for themselves. That being said, it is time for schools to draw a line in the sand: $x$ is a healthy practice to model in front of students, $y$ is not.

Drawing that line begets difficult conversations, because just like SEL, not all adults are self-aware of what is or is not a practice that is healthy and safe for the classroom.

If we agree that teachers are powerful role models and that consuming candy and junk food is an unhealthy practice, then we must also agree that teachers should not model or encourage unhealthy practices in front of students or their families (*even* in the case of fundraising or the school store). When in question, bring it back to your school's Call to Action. Every practice in the school building should help your students Be In the Zone, Be the Solution, and Be Ready to Learn.

## 5. Use SEL as a Whole-class Intervention: Empower Teachers and Students with the Tools to Effectively Self-soothe

SEL is for the whole class, not for the four "problem students" with Individualized Education Plans. *All* students and teachers, regardless of culture, gender, or socio-economic status, experience stress that keeps them from being present in the classroom. Therefore, both students and teachers need to tend to their self-care practices and identify the tools that help them self-soothe without shame or judgment.

Stress manifests itself in different ways in different communities. Some students may be dealing with the pain of living in poverty, some may be dealing with the stressors of a fiercely competitive academic environment, and others may be coping with trauma or tragedy. And naturally, when our students are stressed it creates stress for the teachers and compassion fatigue follows suit. (Also, we can't assume that our teachers are free from pain and trauma.)

What if both students' and teachers' ability to self-soothe was a skill valued in the school community? Instead of shaming or dismissing the practice of self-soothing, what if we cultivated it across the school as part of student and teacher self-care? Self-soothing can be employed not just for the "problem children" or "stressed-out teachers" that "show" that they need it, but as a practice that can help both groups be more present, positive, and engaged. Knowing when and how to self-soothe – how to effectively deal with stress – is a skill necessary for life, from child to adulthood. If we named and practiced effective self-soothing as a life skill, the same way we practice the grammar needed to write a good essay or the math needed to build that backyard fence, would we have less incidents of anorexia, self-harming, or drug abuse among our student populations?

Just as with developing SEL competency, self-care must be made a visible priority across the school building to avoid the teacher burnout, hypertension, and compassion fatigue that comes with navigating our increasingly complex educational system. Teaching is very hard work and I have found that teachers are, by default, nurturers who will "run their tanks on empty" before thinking to take a moment for themselves. Additionally, it is difficult to identify the need for and to prioritize self-care if shame and judgment clouds one's vision.

> "I am so stressed out! Student council elections are on Thursday, grades are due on Friday and I am too busy to take a yoga class. I have too much to do! Anyway, I shouldn't need to take yoga to deal with all that, regardless of what Janice-the-witchy-teacher-down-the-hall says. I shouldn't let her get to me. I am being weak. She is the ridiculous one! She is the one who can't keep her students quiet in the hallway! *She* is the one that needs yoga!!"

What if we shifted the paradigm? If we want our teachers to model self-care and self-soothing, we need our school culture to prioritize these practices and honor their value. The rationale for utilizing Social-Emotional Learning across the school is not only about creating proactive vs. reactive classrooms, it is much larger than that. It is about empowering classroom communities – all students and teachers – with the tools to succeed at life.

To meet this need, I have included the POP Chart Check-In as part of the classroom's morning routine. By giving students a safe space to name their feelings daily we not only begin to omit the judgment and shame associated with the process, we also equip them to proactively deal with their emotions in an informed and controlled way. I also encourage teachers to participate in the POP Chart Check-In to model this practice for their students. It is powerful for students to witness their teacher practicing self-care in an open and transparent way, and it is also the perfect opportunity for the classroom teacher to take care of her needs. For SEL integration across the classroom to be effective, students and teachers must be given the space to step into vulnerability and proactively tackle their stress head-on so they are empowered to be present.

## 6. Be Transparent: Empower Students to Take the Lessons with Them

Define SEL for students. Explain why you are using the Mindful Practices strategies and what shift you expect to see in their behavior (when you come to the activity sections in this book, notice the "Why" introduction of the lessons). Help students find their voices to narrate what their needs are and decode the choices that teachers and administrators make to help them be successful. School is equally a personal and interpersonal pursuit. To be successful, our students must learn to balance the needs of the SELF, such as test taking, with the needs of the SOCIAL, such as managing relationships with peers (notice the SELF and SOCIAL components of the POP Chart). The secret here is to narrate the process for your students without using shaming language. Sometimes a classroom teacher's style is so military-esqe and prescriptive that there is no room for student Self-Awareness to be cultivated. This is one reason some schools often have great test scores and low instances of disciplinary infractions while the students are within the highly structured school environment, but why lifetime achievement numbers – such as high school graduation rates or job retention – don't line up. The students never learned to be self-aware or to self-regulate, they simply learned to comply. By narrating choices for students we are empowering them with the knowledge of what works for them as learners. Often, teachers and administrators are having these conversations behind the scenes: "Let's put Lamar in Ms. Nicole's room next year, because she is a 'go-getter' teacher who does a lot of cooperative learning and he is a kinesthetic learner who has a lot of energy and can't sit for a long time." By sharing this behind-the-scenes logic with both students and their parents, they are empowered with the knowledge of what kind of learning environment is needed for success. I often witness schools making informed decisions about a student's academic trajectory, but not sharing the "Why" of these decisions with the student himself. So, when the student leaves that school (and the community that knows his SEL needs) where he has been successful and moves on to the new school (where his SEL needs are unknown), he is unsuccessful. The student's only take-away is that he knows that he "liked the way that Ms. Nicole taught." He is not empowered with the words to voice his needs as new academic environments present themselves. Transparency is key for students to take ownership of the SEL process and apply the lessons outside of school.

## 7. Multiple Solutions, Same Goal: Use Movement and Stillness

Understanding the connection between trauma, basic needs, fight, flight, or freeze can help the practitioner understand the development of students' SEL skills as well as which tools are most appropriate for students at which times. Sometimes it is movement, not stillness, that is the most accessible and calming practice for students – especially if those students have experienced trauma or live in a community where trauma is pre-valent. As my dear friend Lara Veon, who is a trauma therapist and a member of my Mindful Practices team, articulates:

> Because each child's nervous system is unique, what is relaxing to one student might be activating to another. Stillness, for example, might actually activate the sympathetic nervous system – the stress response – instead of inducing a state of balance or relaxation. In these cases, movement with breath work can be helpful alternatives to bring the parasympathetic nervous system – the rest and relaxa-tion response – back online for a child.

Some students have not experienced trauma, but are negatively impacted by having too little sleep the night before or too much sugar at lunch earlier that afternoon. Or, they simply have different constitutions, just like adults. My husband likes to go to the gym to work off stress, while I like to sit and read a book. To "relax" on vacation, he wants to snowboard down the triple black bowl with our daredevil friends, while I want to gently glide down the green trail with a hot cocoa in one hand. Whether students or adults, what our bodies crave in states of stress or relaxation varies greatly. Therefore, a practitioner that is compassionate, flexible, and responsive, instead of looking for the quick and easy one-size-fits-all SEL model, will have a much more impactful program.

This variance in student need is why the Mindful Practices model includes movement, instead of the standard seated or scripted approach to SEL and mindfulness. If the end goal is for students to be empowered with the tools to move through survival (fight, flight, or freeze) mode when activated, then movement as well as stillness must be included for those learners that find movement more accessible and soothing. It is important that teachers meet students where they are and move their energy accordingly.

When working with different schools across the country, I will often see teachers flip the lights or use shaming language such as "I don't know what is wrong with this class today. You all are acting like crazy people" to attempt to corral a high-energy class. While this strategy may work for a minute or two, the frenetic energy of the class inevitably resurfaces, as the students were not given the tools or opportunity to self-reflect. If we narrate the "Why" to students, they become Self-Aware and can more effectively avoid a retreat to a "fight, flight, or freeze" response when faced with stress or anxiety. (Notice the "Why" prompt in each SEL lesson!)

Wherever they may be, honor where students are and move their energy toward the center, on both an individual and group level. On an energetic scale of 1 to 10, with 1 being Lethargic and 10 being Frenetic, 5 would be Cool, Calm, In the Zone, and Ready to Learn. For a productive learning environment, we need to move both energetic ends of the spectrum toward a focused center of 5.

I have included a few sample lessons below to expand on your classroom's SEL practice, if time permits.

**For lethargic students**, honor where they are by beginning with relaxed energy and shifting to activities with more vibrant energy.

A sample sequence of SELF activities might look like:

Equal Breath (p. 80)
Brain Massage (p. 60)
Yoga Sequence 2 (p. 63)

**For frenetic students**, honor where they are by beginning with dynamic energy and shifting to activities with more centered energy.

A sample sequence of SELF activities might look like:

Partner Mirroring (p. 96)
Yoga Sequence 1 (p. 61)
Ready to Learn Breath (p. 78)

Remember, you can cue a student at any point throughout the day to visit the POP Chart, if she needs to take a moment to relax, focus, and get Ready to Learn.

"Sun-Hi, your energy is at 10 right now. Please visit the POP Chart for 4 minutes, so you can cool down and Self-Regulate. When you have moved your energy closer to a focused 5, you may rejoin your reading group. If you need more time, please let me know."

This process empowers the student with the Self-Awareness needed to Self-Regulate when she feels powerless or out of control. It is important that it is the student that owns the shift in her energy, not the teacher that casually observes, "OK, fine. It looks like you are relaxed, Sun-Hi. Now you can rejoin your reading group."

The same logic applies when your classroom as a group is out of sync. Given the importance of a positive and collaborative climate and culture, bringing the group back together to a place of compassion and Social Harmony is a priority.

**For a low-energy** group, honor where they are by beginning with a reflective energy and shifting to activities with more engaging energy.
A sample sequence of SOCIAL activities might look like:

Positive Paperchain (p. 104)
Cotton Ball Breathing (p. 112)
Shoulder Share (p. 100)

**For a high-energy group,** honor where they are by beginning with an effervescent energy and shifting to activities with more centered energy.
A sample sequence of SOCIAL activities might look like:

Cooperation Circle (p. 86)
Pass the Clap Circle (p. 93)
Pass the Squeeze Circle and One-Word Check-In (p. 91)

## 8. Practice What We Teach: Stay Present, Stay Compassionate, and Avoid Quick Fixes

Creating a safe place for learning means creating a space that is emotionally safe for students and teachers to take risks. Tackling the physical safety of a teacher's classroom space is often the easy part, as that piece is more tangible, more real. One can put her finger on "unsafe objects" or even "unsafe practices" in her classroom. The more difficult piece is the "feeling" or "energy" that creates the climate and culture of the classroom. Teachers must model – and be – compassionate toward themselves and their students.

For example, if there is a student that always seems to disrupt the class and one day he is out sick, the teacher thinking "I am so glad that Jeremy is absent today! I will get so much more done without him in class!" is counterproductive for the teacher as much as it is for that student. It's also only a quick fix, as tomorrow Jeremy will be back and there needs to be a solution that includes Jeremy. Also, although it is often unsaid, this negativity is sensed by the rest of the group and erodes the climate and culture of the classroom. One student being unwelcome in a room does not make the others feel inherently more welcome. However, a classroom that welcomes all, even those that test a teacher's patience, creates a consistent, fair, and compassionate environment for learning – or, as Charlotte Danielson's Domain 2 describes, an "environment of respect and rapport." Ultimately, good teaching is subject to compassion.

An educator's ability to be compassionate – toward herself and her students – is something that is felt immediately upon entering her room. To be Ready to Learn, students need a classroom in which they feel safe and secure. What does safety and security look like in terms of what a teacher provides? In a word: predictability. Students need a set of rules and routines that are predictable so they know exactly what to expect, actualizing that connection between compassion (for SELF and others), mindfulness, and SEL.

Many SEL, character education, or mindfulness programs focus on singular character traits taken out of context, such as "This week is empathy week!" These programs often focus separately on SELF (such as scripted meditation programs) or SOCIAL (such as group restorative programs) instead of bridging the gap between the two. Our Mindful Practices program culminates in a Service Learning Project, which not only authentically connects the SELF and SOCIAL, but also creates more culturally relevant and impactful opportunities for learning. Viewing SEL through this lens enables students to find the balance between the SELF and the SOCIAL in their daily school experience. This reframing guides participants to operate out of compassion for SELF, a skill that, when practiced, can help them operate out of compassion for others as well.

This isn't just for students. Teachers are human: they may get frustrated and frazzled and then fall victim to quick fixes, forgetting that their self-care is an invaluable element of any SEL program's success.

Because the field of SEL lacks robust progress-monitoring tools, the Mindful Practices program includes communication devices (such as Pants on Fire! and Boom Board! as described on pp. 107 and 105) that you can utilize to empower students to ask for help and identify areas of need. Do your homework and trust your gut. Get to know your classroom by avoiding alluring short cuts, such as relying on sparkly technology or cute exercise videos for your "SEL time." Technology and videos alone do not work as effective SEL delivery vehicles, as they don't reinforce personal space or authentic social interaction. Teachers modeling and discussing SEL strategies in real time is one of the most potent implementation tools. Engaging the classroom in experientially learning is the key to SEL, as it helps go beyond reading scenarios about what "should" happen, to dialoguing about and experiencing those scenarios in real time. This level of engagement expands the reach of the SEL practice through peer-to-peer communication, collaboration, problem solving, and other vital life skills. (See Chapter 8 on SEL Stories.)

Marry classroom management and SEL instead of viewing the two practices as disparate elements of the same classroom. For instance, let's say a student enters your class and loudly slams her backpack down. In the old days, the conversation might have sounded something like this:

> "Renata! How dare you interrupt my class by throwing your backpack around! You need to have more respect for your things and the people around you. I don't know what is allowed at home, but that type of childish behavior is not welcome in my class. Next time you come in here and disrupt my class I am sending you down to the principal's office. You understand me?"
>
> "Yeah."
>
> "Look at me when I am speaking to you, Renata, and answer me appropriately. Do you understand me?
>
> "Yes."

Now, the conversation most likely sounds something like:

> "What is going on, Renata? Why did you just slam your backpack down? You are being loud and disruptive."
>
> "Adeela and Dorothy were just super rude to me for no reason. I hate this school! Everyone is rude!"
>
> "OK, well, I know that you are feeling angry and frustrated, but it is not appropriate for you to loudly slam your backpack down while I am trying to start class."
>
> "Fine. Yeah. I won't do it again. Sorry."

As educators, we have an almost instinctive inclination to protect our instructional time. In this case, Renata disrupts the start of our class period, which eats away at our instructional minutes. We don't want this to happen again, so we discuss backpack-throwing with Renata and feel our job is done. We protect the flow of our lesson, and we raise the students' awareness about a problematic behavior so it doesn't happen again. In this scenario, the teacher also tells Renata what Renata is feeling instead of the giving the student the space to find her voice. Is this Social-Emotional Learning?

To move our students through Self-Awareness to Self-Regulation onto Social Awareness to the balance between Self-Efficacy and Social Harmony, the conversation needs to sound something like this:

"Renata, I noticed that you slammed your backpack down. Take a moment to Pause and find your breath. Would you like to share what is going on?"

"No. [pause] I mean, yeah. Sure. [pause] Adeela and Dorothy were just super rude to me for no reason."

"OK, so why did you slam your backpack down?"

"Um. I dunno."

"Can you Own what you are feeling?"

"I dunno. [pause] Frustrated. Angry. I mean everyone in this school is super rude and I hate it."

"It is OK to feel frustrated and angry. But it is not OK to be disruptive when we are starting our class or to make generalizations about others. So, next time you are angry or frustrated what can you Practice instead of slamming your backpack down?"

"Um. … I dunno."

"Well, when you are at school or at home … What calms you down? What activities from our POP Chart do you practice during our morning check-in to help you be present and focused?"

"Well, sometimes I like to doodle when I am upset. Or, I practice Ready to Learn Breath when I lose my cool."

"OK, so how about next time you are angry or frustrated you take a moment to sit down, practice a few Ready to Learn Breaths and doodle instead of throwing your backpack around. Will that work?"

"Yeah. I think so. I mean, I can try it. And sorry about the backpack thing. I didn't mean to disrupt the class."

"Thank you for apologizing. I understand. The most important thing is that you are empowered with a solution next time you are upset."

"Yeah. Thanks, Mr. Jakubowski."

"Any time, Renata. Reflecting and finding a way to Be the Solution is all part of the Social-Emotional Learning process."

# 2

# Getting Started: Introducing Social-Emotional Learning and Setting Up Your Classroom

Intentionality is key to creating an impactful classroom SEL program. The mindful set-up of the classroom environment is a critical piece in the program's success, as it creates a safe environment in which learning takes place. When done well, the classroom culture is palpable; you can see it, hear it and feel it as soon as you enter the room. A Call to Action, such as Being In the Zone, Being the Solution, or Being Ready to Learn, becomes the lens through which students view their school experience.

Here are five steps to lay the groundwork before you begin implementation with your students:

1.  Build your own SEL competency and mastery, as a practitioner. Make time for reflection, self-care, and expanding your learning. Reflect on your needs as a classroom teacher. What are the times each day when the climate and culture of your classroom is compromised? What negatively impacts your Self-Efficacy and that of your students?
2.  Create a Call to Action, such as Being In the Zone, Being the Solution, or Being Ready to Learn. Implement this with fidelity so that it becomes the lens through which your students view their school

experience. (As you read, note the Be the Solution behavioral expectations consistently messaged throughout the Extended Scripts.)

3. Create an implementation schedule. The morning routine each day includes a check-in and visit to the POP Chart. Every Monday, teach your weekly SEL Story; during the rest of the week, utilize your POP Chart to constructively harness and shift student energy. Make sure your room is laid out so that students can feel emotionally and physically safe moving their bodies and exploring their breath.

4. Set up your SEL Classroom (see Figures 2.1 and 2.2). Designate bulletin boards, wipe boards, and wall space in your classroom for your SEL tools (which will be discussed below): a POP Chart, your signed Agreements poster, Boom Board!, Pants on Fire!, and space for supplies including sticky notes, pencils, the Thumbs-Up/Thumbs-Down Box, and a Talking Stick.

5. Be consistent! Whether you use verbal cues or non-verbal ones, such as dimming the lights or playing music, to move student attention, reflect on which cues work best for you and implement with fidelity.

**Figure 2.1** The SEL classroom

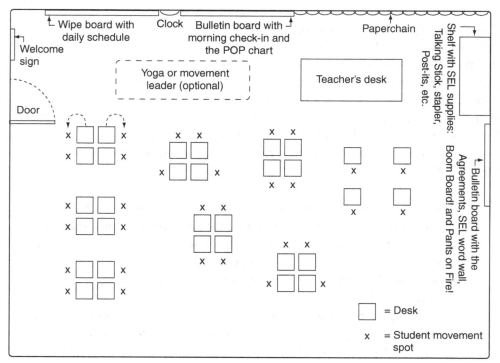

**Figure 2.2** The SEL wall

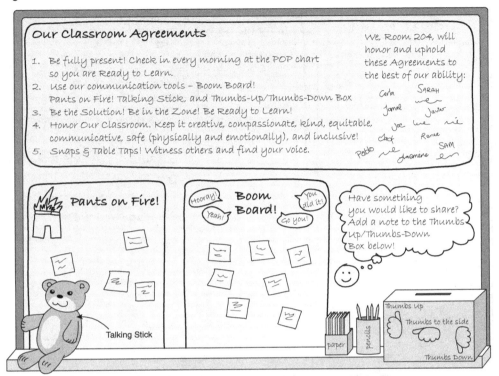

## Defining SEL and Establishing Protocols and Procedures

Once the classroom has been set up, it is important to take the time to walk students through their daily routine prior to starting instruction. Model the strategies for the students, demonstrating how to perform a morning check-in, use an activity in the POP Chart, add a sticky note to the Boom Board!, etc. As Harry Wong points out in his work, *The First Days of School*, consistently practiced classroom routines at the start of the school year can be the key to student success. Have activities posted clearly as part of your daily schedule (Figure 2.3). Reinforce an emotionally and physical safe classroom environment by being transparent and consistent.

School schedules can look very different from district to district. Some larger districts, for example Chicago Public Schools, are predominantly K–8 buildings, while other districts have early childhood centers and middle schools. I have sketched out an easily adaptable sample implementation model on the next page.

**Figure 2.3** Daily SEL schedule

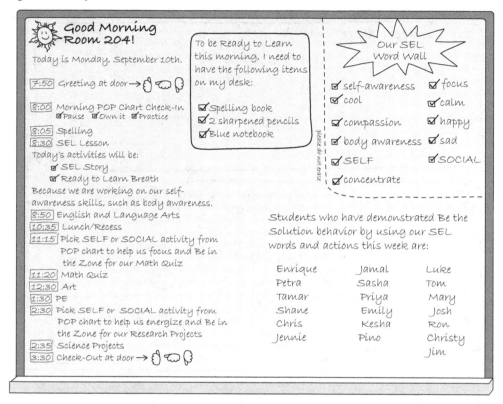

Your classroom SEL practice every Monday:

1. A Morning POP Chart Check-In
2. A Social-Emotional Learning Story

Your classroom SEL practice, Tuesday–Friday:

1. A Morning POP Chart Check-In
2. A SELF or SOCIAL activity added to your POP Chart

Additionally, the POP Chart activities are there at any time if you need your class to Get In the Zone, or if individual students need a break to relax, energize, or focus (see Figure 2.4).

When the new activity is learned, a card for that activity is added to the POP Chart. That way, the activity can be practiced again throughout the week, during both the morning check-in (if a student identifies a need for herself) or throughout the day (if the teacher identifies a need for the group). To implement with fidelity, the recommended dosage or intervention is 10–25 minutes per day, including the Morning POP Chart Check-In.

**Figure 2.4** POP chart

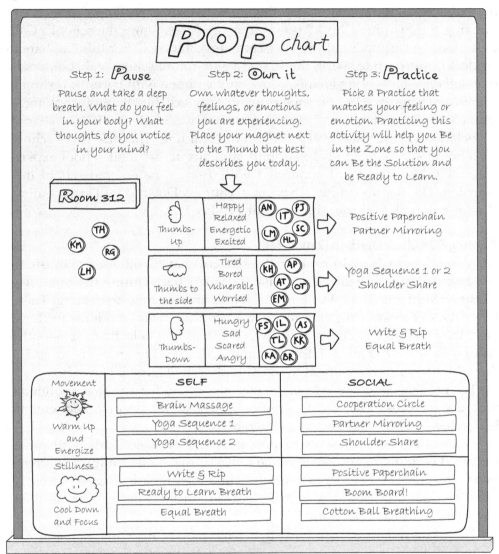

## What Does Implementation Look Like?

### Starting the School Day

To take a cue from one of our terrific school partners, Chicago International Charter School West Belden, I recommend that all school stakeholders check in with students as they enter the building at the start of each school day. For instance, from 7:45 am to 7:55 am, teachers, administrators, deans, social workers, parent volunteers, custodians, and lunchroom staff are in the hallways with students, greeting them warmly, making eye contact, utilizing the "Thumb Check" (see below), and messaging the school's Call to Action. The school's culture is visceral, real, and rich. For this "all hands on deck" approach to work, the shared value for all school stakeholders is that *nothing* – answering emails, being on the phone with parents, texting a friend, entering grades, or squeezing in that last bit of photocopying – trumps the importance of being present for the students. It is a shared expectation for each and every adult in the building. This also gives school stakeholders a chance to help support students across their school experience. "Hi, Ms. Jimenez. I connected with Taki as he entered school this morning. He mentioned he is having a Thumbs Down day. Do you mind checking in with him later during your PE class?"

## Morning POP Chart Check-In (2 minutes)

For your class's Check-In routine, the students have 2 minutes of music to get their materials organized and visit the POP Chart. During the 2 minutes of music, students first PAUSE to check in with how they are feeling. Then, they OWN IT by moving their magnets to indicate their emotions/feelings. Last, they choose an activity to PRACTICE that will help them self-soothe and be Ready to Learn for the day ahead. Encourage students to add a thought, concern, or comment to the Thumbs-Up/Thumbs-Down box.

For English language learners or students or students with exceptionalities, use pictures of faces with emotions and feelings (Happy, Sad, etc.) in lieu of the Thumbs-Up/Thumbs-Down box.

Depending on your school's policy on cell phones, iPads, and other screens, I would strongly recommend that you make this 2 minutes "screen free." The goal is for students to unplug, find their breath, and be present.

When the music is over, the students are at their desks with all their materials out, Ready to Learn.

For those individual students that have moved their magnets but are having a difficult time finding a PRACTICE, the teachers may take a moment during the morning routine to check in with the students and ask them a series of questions such as, "Where do you feel that emotion in your body? When are other times that you feel that way? Looking at our POP Chart, what is a strategy you can PRACTICE – either SELF or SOCIAL – to be Ready to Learn for the day?"

It is recommended that the teacher set clear expectations with students, to help ensure that the morning POP Chart Check-In routine is a smooth, fluid, and safe process. Whole-class implementation (Tier 1) is preferred, with extended time in the POP Chart for students with exceptionalities or who need assistance modifying their behavior. These additional minutes can be added to the morning POP Chart Check-In to give students extra processing time.

### Thumb Check: The Importance of Checking in with Students Throughout the Day

At multiple points throughout the day, the teacher may ask the classroom for a "Thumb Check" to check in with students and gauge their energy or emotions. The teacher simply signals the students to hold their thumbs against their chests, which is quick and easy if the class is transitioning between activities, if there is a field trip or a school assembly, or if energy levels fluctuate throughout the day.

Thumbs-Up = I'm great!
Thumbs to the Side = Mweh. I'm OK.
Thumbs-Down = I'm having a bad day.

Let the students know that you will always try to individually check in with them, if you can. Invite them to share thoughts, feelings, and emotions in the Thumbs-Up/Thumbs-Down Box (a small box in which students can submit notes; see Figure 2.2, p. 35). Also, make sure you review Talking Stick procedures (p. 110) as some of your students may want to share ideas with the class.

Offer the POP Chart as a solution to those students who need help Being In the Zone throughout the day or when the whole class needs help being Ready to Learn. Giving the classroom community multiple methods to "check-in" each day demonstrates that the teacher is invested in providing opportunities for all students to practice naming, identifying, and proactively dealing with emotions. This practice is powerful, as it is used for the students' initial morning POP Chart Check-In (by putting their magnet next to the Thumb that indicates how they are feeling) as well by the teacher for random "Thumb Checks" each day. Encourage all school stakeholders, parents, administrators, staff, and community members to check in with students as part of the morning greeting and at any point over the course of the school day with a quick "Thumb Check." Utilize your Call to Action messaging to give students multiple opportunities throughout the day to visit the POP Chart when they need to Be In the Zone, focus, and be Ready to Learn. Additionally, when behavioral infractions occur, empower students to Be the Solution and select an activity from the POP Chart to help shift the energy of their classroom community so that they can be attentive and present learners.

## Be the Solution: POP Chart Scenarios for the Classroom Community

### 8:30 am: Breathwork Activity before Reading Groups

It is the week before Winter Break and the teacher notices her class is unusually hyper and can't get focused on reading. Instead of using shaming language such as "I cannot believe how crazy this class is today!" the teacher recruits the students' help in finding a solution.

"OK, Room [x], I notice we have a lot of extra energy this morning. Let's Be the Solution and use an SEL activity to be present, focus, and get Ready to Learn. [Student name], thank you for actively listening with your eyes on me. Can you please go to our POP Chart and select an activity that will help our class settle down and focus? [Student choses activity. Teacher again reinforces positive behavior by choosing a student to lead the class through the activity.] Nicely done, Room [x]. I see students that are In the Zone and Ready to Learn! Before we transition back to reading, I would like to get a one-word check-in from a few students. I am looking for students who are sitting with feet flat on the floor, eyes on me, and respecting their neighbor's personal space. [Teacher calls on two or three students to share a quick word with the room on how they are feeling, for example "calm" or "relaxed."]

### 11:15 am: Physical Movement After Lunch

Outdoor recess has been canceled today because of a snowstorm. The teacher is giving a big test in 5 minutes and knows her students would benefit from a bit of yoga or physical movement to let off some extra stress and anxiety. "Our class has a lot of excess energy that is keeping us from being focused and Ready to Learn. Thank you for demonstrating Be the Solution behavior, Gina, by sitting with feet flat on the floor, eyes on me, respecting your neighbor's personal space. Will you go to the POP Chart and choose an activity to help our class get In the Zone for our big test?"

### 2:30 pm: Energizing Activity

"Room [x], I notice our energy is low, and we still have our research projects to work on this afternoon. Let's Be the Solution and use an SEL activity to energize our bodies and get Ready to Learn. [Student name], thank you for actively listening with your eyes on me. Can you please go to our POP Chart and select an activity that will help energize our class and stimulate our brains? [Student chooses activity. Teacher again reinforces positive behavior by choosing a new student to lead the class through the selected activity.] Nicely done, Room [x]. Now, we are energized and ready to tackle our research projects!"

## Be the Solution: POP Chart Procedures for the Individual Student

Next to the POP Chart, clearly post procedures for taking a break along with an SEL word wall and the classroom communication tools, Boom Board! (p. 105), Pants on Fire! (p. 107), and the Thumbs-Up/Thumbs-Down Box (see Figure 2.2). Remember that classical music or jazz in the background can help with transitions. This practice can be especially important at the beginning of the year when learning to be present in quiet surroundings can be an awkward and uncomfortable process for many students, especially those that have experienced trauma.

The following procedures apply to the students that visit the POP Chart at any time throughout your class to cool down, focus, and be Ready to Learn. Students may request to visit the POP Chart after a fight on the playground or a stressful afternoon. Establish your expectations for POP Chart behavior (i.e. Do students raise their hand to ask if they can get out of their seats and walk over to the POP Chart? What is the procedure if more than one student wants to visit the POP Chart at a time? Are there any times, such as during a test, when the POP Chart is closed to visitors?)

Step 1: Sit facing the POP Chart and set the timer for 2 minutes. [Encourage students to sit with their backs to the class; that way they can disconnect from the room. Students should not feel as if they are being watched and should not be easily able to distract other students.]

Step 2: Choose one activity to practice for the entire 2 minutes.

Step 3: When the timer goes off, stop the activity.

Step 4: Complete your Exit Slip.

Step 5: Hand your Exit Slip to the teacher and rejoin our class.

★ **Teacher Tip:** Have Exit Slips printed out and placed next to the POP Chart with writing utensils. On each slip is space for the student's name, the date, and the SEL activity chosen. To complete the Exit Slip, the student writes 1–2 sentences on how x activity helped him or her get back In the Zone. Additional Exit Slip questions may include, "Is there anything you want to add to the Thumbs-Down/Thumbs-Up Box today?" or "How can you self-soothe and Be the Solution when you are at recess, at home, or in another classroom that does not have a POP Chart?" Keep the Exit Slips brief so that students can completely them quickly and return to class.

## Classroom Agreements for SEL

Below are sample Agreements to use as a platform to build consensus among your students. The Agreements are implemented to create an emotionally and physically safe place for communication and to guarantee equity of voice. Once revised, the Agreements should be signed by all class members, laminated, and hung next to the POP Chart (see Figure 2.2).

1.  **Be fully present! Check in every morning so you are Ready to Learn.**
    ◆ Pause, Own It, and Practice (POP Chart).
2.  **Use our communication tools.**
    ◆ Boom Board! Pants on Fire! Thumbs-Up/Thumbs-Down Box and Talking Stick. Use your words. Find your voice.
3.  **Be the Solution.**
    ◆ Do your actions help our class to Be In the Zone and Ready to Learn at all times? Be the Solution behavior = sitting up tall, feet flat on the floor, hands folded on the desk, and eyes on the speaker.
4.  **Honor our classroom.**
    ◆ Keep it creative, compassionate, kind, equitable, communicative, safe (physically and emotionally), and inclusive!
5.  ***Snaps* and Table Taps**
    ◆ Positively witness your peers and hold each other accountable.

> ★ **Teacher Tip:** *Snaps* = students snap three times in the air when they agree with the student speaking. Table Taps = students tap their fingers on the table if someone breaks the Agreements or says something disrespectful such as "All fifth graders are lazy."

If you would also like to create Agreements for individual activities, as seen in Write and Rip (p. 70) and Cooperation Circle (p. 86), use the script below to build consensus and safety. Create the Agreements after the directions of the activity have been introduced, but prior to when the activity itself begins.

## Consensus-building and Creating the Agreements

Before we begin [x activity], I need to find a student who is demonstrating our Be the Solution behavior by sitting up tall, with two feet flat on the floor, hands folded, and respecting his neighbor's personal space, who can restate our new activity in his own words. [Teacher calls on student demonstrating the expectations. Student restates activity.]

Thank you, [student name]. Room [x], do we see any potential problems with implementing this activity? [Teacher calls on one or two students to discuss potential pitfalls.]

Thank you, [student names]. So, now that we know where the problems may occur, how can we Be the Solution? What Agreements do we need to make for the activity to be physically and emotionally safe for all? What are the consequences if the Agreements are broken?

★ **Teacher Tip:** For this consensus-building strategy to be successful, it is imperative that you consistently uphold the Agreements and enforce the consequences. If a class member violates the Agreements, then the consequences must be implemented, or else the students will no longer trust that the classroom environment is safe.

We have time for [x number of] students to share their thoughts. Before we share, let's remember to listen intently to others, accept others' opinions, and be careful not to interrupt our classmates.

[Teacher calls on students and writes the Agreements and consequences on the board. This is also the perfect time for the teacher to suggest modifications to the activity for students with limited physical mobility, students with self-esteem challenges, students who are deaf and hard of hearing, English language learners, and students with exceptionalities.]

Thank you, [student names]. Now that we have our Agreements and consequences on the board, let's Check for Understanding.* Please raise your right hand in the air. A "high five" hand tells me you understand the activity, our Agreements, and the consequences if the Agreements are broken, and you are all set to begin. Two fingers in the air, or a peace sign, tells me that you have a question or comment that needs to be addressed before we begin. A fist in the air tells me that you are unsure and you are not ready to begin, which is

OK. It is important that we have created a physically and emotionally safe classroom environment for our activity to take place.

[Teacher reads room and responds appropriately to student needs by answering questions, restating activity, building consensus, etc.]

Thank you, Room [x], for sharing your thoughts respectfully and thoughtfully. I witnessed students actively listening to their peers. Well done! Now, let's move on to our activity, [x]!

* Adapted from Doug Lemov's Check for Understanding.

## Introducing SEL to Your Students: Days 1–3

Below are three days of scripted lessons for introducing SEL, the morning check-in, the POP Chart, Boom Board!, and other components of your classroom. Taking the time to pre-teach the concepts and create a safe space for learning is essential to the success of any SEL program. Diving immediately into the activities, without taking the time to lay the foundation, will potentially leave the students feeling confused and vulnerable. As with the other scripted lessons in this book, it is *not* recommended that you read the script aloud word for word, as that would not help develop your competency as a practitioner. Instead, the script is meant to be a reflective guide that provides a solid idea of how the content is framed, paced, and managed. Read the script a few times, take notes, and then make it your own.

For additional tips on how to reinforce the concepts of personal space and safe touch with your students, please see the section on "Be the Solution: educator questions from the field" in the Appendix.

## Day 1: Defining SEL and Classroom Practices for Your Students

[To cue students that their SEL time is going to start, the teacher begins the music.]

Room [x], I have started the music. When the song is over, I need to see students at their desks demonstrating our Be the Solution behavior by sitting up tall, with two feet flat on the floor, respecting their neighbors' personal space.

[Teacher stops music, students are in seats ready to begin.] Thank you for following directions and being in your seats, Ready to Learn, when the song was over. Great job, class!

I am excited, because this week begins our Social-Emotional Learning program! Every Monday we will start our week with a

Social-Emotional Learning or SEL lesson for our class! [Teacher writes Social-Emotional Learning on the board.]

I am looking for students with Be the Solution behavior to make a prediction of the definition of Social-Emotional Learning. [Teacher calls on students demonstrating the expectations. Students guess definition of SEL. Teacher writes keywords on the board.]

> ★ **Teacher Tip:** As recommended previously, when your students behave inappropriately, you are encouraged to engage them in a discussion about Being the Solution or Being In the Zone, or whatever Call to Action you are using in your classroom. Ask them if their behavior "moves them toward our classroom goal of being Ready to Learn." "Ready to Learn" is framed as the SEL goal of our classroom; "Being the Solution" or "Being In the Zone" is messaged as the method to help us reach our shared goal.

I see eyes on me and great active listening, Room [x]! Thank you! Now, let's break down the name Social-Emotional Learning. *Social* is interacting with your classmates, friends, family, teachers, adults at school and in your community! So, to help us remember *Social* let's stretch our arms out wide, like this [teacher stretches arms out wide, students follow].

*Emotional* refers to all the feelings and emotions we experience, when we are by ourselves and when we are socializing with others. Like how it is important to be compassionate, or kind to ourselves, so then we can learn to be compassionate or kind to others. To help us remember *Emotional*, we will put two hands over our hearts [teacher models, students follow].

The last part of the name is *Learning*: Social-Emotional Learning; learning about our behavior and interactions with others along with our feelings and emotions. But, since this is a school, the word *Learning* also has a special meaning. Here, *Learning* can also mean that if our behavior, emotions, and interactions with others are positive, they can help us Be the Solution and be Ready to Learn. So, for the word *Learning*, let's put hands on the top of our heads [teacher models, students follow].

Let's practice the entire sequence two times together: *Social* [teacher and students stretch their arms out wide], *Emotional* [teacher and students put two hands over their hearts], *Learning* [teacher and students put hands on the top of their heads].

Nice job, Room [x]! I see everyone participating and trying their best! Let's practice our Social-Emotional Learning sequence one more time: *Social* [teacher and students stretch their arms out wide], *Emotional* [teacher and students put two hands over their hearts], *Learning* [teacher and students put hands on the top of their heads]. Great job, everyone!

Social-Emotional Learning is the process through which we develop Self-Awareness – being aware of how emotions and feelings affect our bodies and minds and influence how we make decisions. Social-Emotional Learning helps us look at how the consequences of our actions affect our classmates, our school, and ourselves. By studying Social-Emotional Learning, we can self-regulate – or make more positive, kind choices about our behavior – so that we can be compassionate toward others and ourselves.

Social-Emotional Learning helps us understand our emotions so we can calm down, focus, and Be the Solution instead of the problem, so we are always Ready to Learn!

All the activities that we learn during our Social-Emotional Learning time will be added to our POP Chart in either the SELF or SOCIAL column. The SELF activities are strategies that we use personally, or as individuals. The SOCIAL activities are strategies that help us work better as a group, or interpersonally. School is a place where we need to work on our SELF skills, such as taking a test or resolving a conflict with a friend, and our SOCIAL skills, such as working as a team or behaving well when our class has a substitute teacher. You will also notice that some activities help us warm up and energize (teacher motions to the chart), while other activities help us cool down and focus. The activities, or strategies, are broken up in this way on the chart so that we can cultivate Self-Awareness and get to know ourselves, or build Social Awareness and learn how our energy and actions impact our classroom community.

★ **Teacher Tip:** At this point, I would recommend introducing students to "Life: The Game of Social-Emotional Learning" (Figure 2.5) or the Mindful Practices model (Figure 1.2) so that they begin to understand the progression from basic needs ("fight, flight, or freeze") to the balance between Self-Efficacy and Social Harmony. While you may not get through the entire game or chart in this first lesson, this is a great moment to pre-teach concepts and/or add words and concepts to your SEL word wall.

The POP on our chart stands for "Pause – Own It – and Practice." This is how we approach our feelings and emotions during our morning check-in routine each day. [Teacher walks to center and points to pocket chart.] Let's take a look at our POP Chart.

In the morning, we go to the POP Chart as part of our daily routine. First, you will PAUSE to notice what you are feeling. Then, you OWN what you are feeling, by placing your magnet next to the thumb that best depicts your emotion that day. Last, you will find a PRACTICE that best meets your emotional needs so you can get In the Zone and be Ready to Learn.

For instance, let's say you are checking in tomorrow morning, after you had a fight with your sister at breakfast. You PAUSE and notice that the emotion you are coming to school with is *anger*, because you are still upset about the fight. So, you OWN your emotions and place your magnet next to the Thumbs Down, which communicates to me and your classmates that you are upset. [Teacher demonstrates.]

Next, you will find which activities in the PRACTICE column can help you self-soothe and calm down. Self-soothing is when you take a moment to be kind and compassionate with yourself. When we take a moment to be kind to ourselves, it is easier to let go of anger and be Ready to Learn.

It is important that you always check in in the morning by going to the POP Chart. That way, you always have an opportunity to PAUSE and name the emotion you are feeling, instead of carrying it with you all day. By OWNING it you are able to find the right SEL tool to PRACTICE, so that you can cool down, focus, and be Ready to Learn.

Let's review! Step 1 is PAUSE and notice what you are feeling in the body and in the mind. Step 2 is OWN IT, whatever you are feeling in the body and in the mind. Put your magnet by the Thumbs-Up, Thumbs-to-the-Side, or Thumbs-Down picture that best describes where you are today. Step 3, PRACTICE the activity

**Figure 2.5** Life: The Game of Social-Emotional Learning

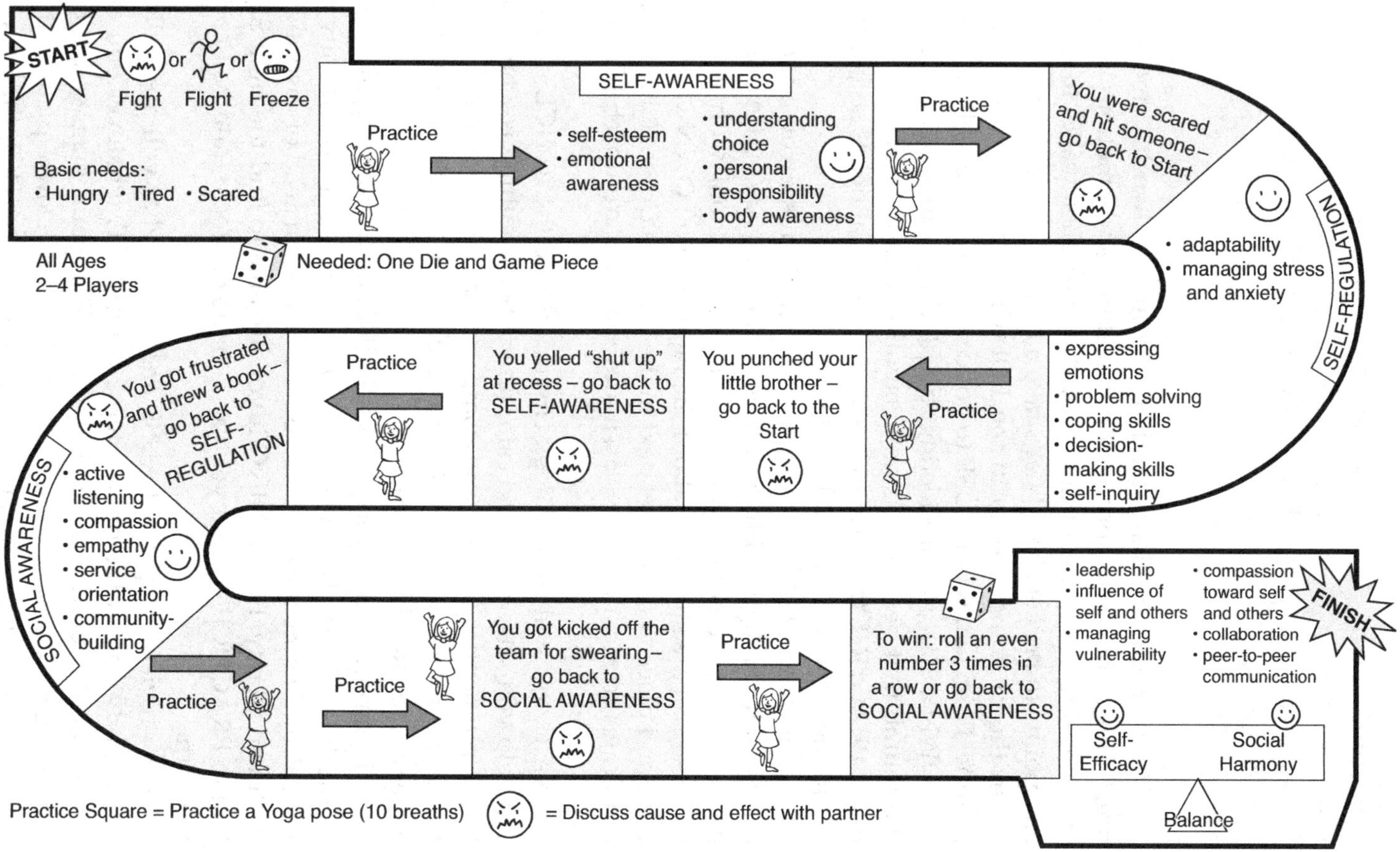

Practice Square = Practice a Yoga pose (10 breaths)    (☺) = Discuss cause and effect with partner

on the POP Chart that will help you self-soothe, focus, and be Ready to Learn.

Sometimes, I will say that our class needs to "Get In the Zone" and we will practice an activity together. At other times, I might ask that you go to the POP Chart on your own to practice an activity, before you rejoin the group. For instance, I might say, "Julio, I notice you are having a difficult time honoring your neighbor's personal space. Please go to the POP Chart to choose an activity to help you focus and get Ready to Learn." Then, Julio will choose an activity that will help him focus and make more positive choices. When Julio feels he is Ready to Learn, he will rejoin our class.

As I mentioned before, we will add a new activity to the POP Chart each week during Monday's SEL time. There are three different situations when we can visit the POP Chart to practice those activities.

The first is during our morning check-in routine, when we all PAUSE to notice what we are feeling, OWN what we are feeling by naming the feeling or emotion, and PRACTICE an activity that can help us relax, self-soothe, and be Ready to Learn.

The second is any time our class needs to Be the Solution, and we do an activity together to focus and Be In the Zone.

The third is any time you need to take a moment to regulate your behavior and Be the Solution, you raise your hand and ask to go to the POP Chart.

Let's also take a look at our Boom Board!, Pants on Fire!, Talking Stick, Paperchain, the Agreements, and our SEL word wall. These are tools we will develop throughout the year as we develop our practices together.

The POP Chart is always here when you need an individual break to help you cool down and be in control of your emotions. Social-Emotional Learning helps us positively deal with our emotions, both personally and interpersonally, so that we can always Be the Solution and be Ready to Learn. Remember, you can always practice your SEL tools at home too!

[Teacher walks to center and points to pocket chart.] I am looking for two volunteers with Be the Solution behavior to tell me the three different ways we can use the POP Chart. [Teacher calls on students demonstrating the expectations.]

Nicely done, [student names]. Remember, students, you are the Solution. You are in charge of your own behavior!

## Day 2: Reviewing SEL

[To cue students that their SEL time is going to start, the teacher begins the music.]

Room [x], I have started the music. When the song is over, I need to see students at their desks demonstrating our Be the Solution behavior by sitting up tall, with two feet flat on the floor, hands folded, and respecting their neighbor's personal space.

[Teacher stops music, students are in seats, with feet flat on the floor, hands folded, ready to begin.] Thank you for following directions and being in your seats, Ready to Learn, when the song was over. Great job, class!

Last week we learned about Social-Emotional Learning or SEL. I am looking for students with Be the Solution behavior to tell me, in their own words, what Social-Emotional Learning is. [Teacher calls on students demonstrating the expectations. Students restate definition of SEL. Teacher writes keywords on the board.]

Very nice, Room [x]! Let's practice our Social-Emotional Learning sequence together: *Social* [teacher and students stretch their arms out wide], *Emotional* [teacher and students put one hand over their hearts, then give themselves a hug], *Learning* [teacher and students put hands on the top of their heads]. I am looking for a student who is demonstrating our Be the Solution behavior by sitting up tall, with two feet flat on the floor, hands folded, and respecting his neighbor's personal space, who can come to the front of the room and lead our class through our SEL sequence. [Teacher chooses student, student leads class through sequence.] Great job, everyone! Let's try that one more time! [Student leads class through sequence again.]

Let's take a look at this Social-Emotional Learning diagram. [Teacher draws simple diagram on board; see Figure 1.2.] Can I have a volunteer to explain the diagram to me? Nicely done, [student name]!

Nice work, Room [x]. I saw students respecting their neighbor's personal space and actively following our class leader. Let's remember that Social-Emotional Learning is the process by which we develop Self-Awareness – how emotions and feelings affect our bodies and minds – and influence how we make decisions. Social-Emotional Learning helps us look at how the consequences of our actions affect our classmates, our school, and ourselves. By studying

Social-Emotional Learning, we can Self-Regulate – or make more positive, kind choices about our behavior – so that we can be compassionate toward ourselves and others. Social-Emotional Learning helps us understand our emotions so we can calm down, focus, and Be the Solution so we are always Ready to Learn!

Let's take a moment to review our Social-Emotional Learning morning POP Chart Check-In! Step 1 is to PAUSE and notice what you are feeling in the body and in the mind. Step 2 is to OWN It by placing your magnet by the Thumbs-Up/Thumbs-Down that best describes your emotion. Step 3, PRACTICE the activity on the POP Chart that will help you self-soothe, focus, and be Ready to Learn.

Let's also take this opportunity to discuss the difference between the activities in the SELF and SOCIAL columns on the POP Chart. The SELF activities are strategies that we use personally, or as individuals. The SOCIAL activities are strategies that help us work better as a group, or interpersonally. School is a place where we need to work on our SELF skills, such as when we are stressed about a quiz or worried about a friend, and our SOCIAL skills, such as when are working with others on a project or our class needs to improve our lunchroom behavior. You will also notice that some activities help us warm up and energize (teacher motions to the chart), while other activities help us cool down and focus. Some of us like movement to help us Get In the Zone, and some of us like breathing or relaxation activities to help us Get In the Zone. Each of us is built differently and has different needs. The most important thing is to be aware of our needs so that we can regulate our behavior and make positive choices. The activities, or strategies, are broken up in this way on the chart so that we can choose the activity that is the best fit for our classmates or us on that particular day.

★ **Teacher Tip:** At this point, I would recommend re-introducing students to "Life: The Game of Social-Emotional Learning" (Figure 2.5) or the Mindful Practices model (Figure 1.2) so that they can further understand the progression from Basic Needs ("fight, flight, or freeze") to the balance between Self-Efficacy and Social Harmony. Depending on your class, you may be able to expand on your game or discussion from the introductory lesson and add additional words and concepts to your SEL word wall.

I am now looking for students with Be the Solution behavior to tell me the three ways we practice SEL in Room [x]. [Teacher calls on students. Students give examples of how the POP Chart can be utilized throughout the day.] Well done, Room [x]!

> ★ **Teacher Tip:** As recommended previously, when your students behave inappropriately, you are encouraged to engage them in a discussion about Being the Solution or Being In the Zone, or whatever Call to Action you are using in your classroom. Ask them if their behavior "moves them toward our classroom goal of being Ready to Learn." "Ready to Learn" is framed as the SEL goal of our classroom. "Being the Solution" or "Being In the Zone" is messaged as the method to help us reach our shared goal.

After we learn a new Social-Emotional Learning activity, we will write it on a sentence strip and add it to our POP Chart, so that we can practice it any time our class needs help controlling our behavior, dealing with a stressful situation or getting along with peers. The POP Chart is here to help us positively deal with our emotions, so that we can always Be the Solution and be Ready to Learn.

Let's review the activities in our POP Chart. [Teacher walks over to center and names activities.] Practicing these activities as part of our morning check-in routine helps us remember that we are the Solution. We are in charge of our own behavior.

Before we practice our SEL activity, I am looking for a student who is demonstrating our Be the Solution behavior by sitting up tall, with two feet flat on the floor, hands folded, and respecting her neighbor's personal space, who can tell me what Social-Emotional Learning is her own words. [Teacher chooses one student to restate definition.] Now, may I have another volunteer to explain why we need Social-Emotional Learning in school? [Teacher chooses another student to share their thoughts.] May I have one more student explain how our POP Chart can help us Be In the Zone, Be the Solution and Be Ready to Learn? [Teacher chooses one last student to share.]

## Day 3: Reviewing the Definition of SEL

[To cue students that their SEL time is going to start, the teacher begins the music.]

Room [x], I have started the music. When the song is over, I need to see students at their desks demonstrating our Be the Solution behavior by sitting up tall, with two feet flat on the floor, hands folded, and respecting their neighbor's personal space.

[Teacher stops music, students are in seats, with feet flat on the floor, hands folded, ready to begin.] Thank you for following directions and being in your seats, Ready to Learn, when the song was over. Great job, class!

These last few weeks we have learned about Social-Emotional Learning or SEL. I am looking for students with Be the Solution behavior to tell me, in their own words, what Social-Emotional Learning is. [Teacher calls on students demonstrating the expectations. Students restate definition of SEL. Teacher writes keywords on the board.] Well done, Room [x]!

I am now looking for students with Be the Solution behavior to tell me the three ways we practice SEL in Room [x]. [Teacher calls on students. Students give examples of different ways to utilize the POP Chart throughout the day.]

Well done, Room [x]. Let's practice our Social-Emotional Learning sequence together: *Social* [teacher and students stretch their arms out wide], *Emotional* [teacher and students put one hand over their hearts, then give themselves a hug], *Learning* [teacher and students put hands on the top of their heads]. I am looking for a student who is demonstrating our Be the Solution behavior by sitting up tall, with two feet flat on the floor, hands folded, and respecting her neighbor's personal space, who can come to the front of the room and lead our class through our SEL sequence. [Teacher chooses student, student leads class through sequence.] Great job, everyone! Let's try that one more time! [Student leads class through sequence again.]

Nice work, Room [x]. I saw students respecting their neighbor's personal space and paying attention to our class leader.

Very nice, Room [x]! Let's remember that Social-Emotional Learning is the process through which we develop Self-Awareness – how emotions and feelings affect our bodies and minds – and influence how we make decisions. Social-Emotional Learning helps us look at how the consequences of our actions impact our classmates, our school, and ourselves. By studying Social-Emotional Learning, we can self-regulate – or make more positive, kind choices about our behavior – so that we can be compassionate toward others and ourselves. Social-Emotional Learning helps us understand our emotions so we can calm down, focus, and Be the Solution instead of the problem so we are always Ready to Learn!

Let's remember that the SELF activities on the POP Chart are the strategies that we use personally, or as individuals. The SOCIAL activities on the POP Chart are strategies that help us work better as a group, or interpersonally. School is a place where we need to cultivate our SELF skills and our SOCIAL skills to be successful learners. You will also notice that some activities help us warm up and energize (teacher motions to the chart), while other activities help us cool down and focus. Some of us like movement to help us Get In the Zone, and some of us like breathing or relaxation activities to help us Get In the Zone. Each of us is built differently and has different needs. The most important thing is to be aware of our needs so that we can regulate our behavior and make positive choices. The activities, or strategies, are broken up in this way on the chart so that we can choose the activity that is the best fit for our classmates or ourselves on that particular day. Remember, we can always practice our SEL tools at home too, if we are ever feeling stressed, anxious, or worried!

★ **Teacher Tip:** At this point, I would recommend having students play "Life: The Game of Social-Emotional Learning" (Figure 2.5) or look at the Mindful Practices model (Figure 1.2) so that they can further understand the progression from Basic Needs ("fight, flight, or freeze") to the balance between Self-Efficacy and Social Harmony. Depending on your class, you may be able to continue to expand on your game or discussion and add additional words and concepts to your SEL word wall.

Additionally, as recommended previously, when your students behave inappropriately, you are encouraged to engage them in a discussion about Being the Solution or Being In the Zone, or whatever Call to Action you are using in your classroom. Ask them if their behavior "moves them toward our classroom goal of being Ready to Learn." "Ready to Learn" is framed as the SEL goal of our classroom. "Being the Solution" or "Being In the Zone" is messaged as the method to help us reach our shared goal.

# 3

# Using the Activities and Your POP Chart

The Mindful Practices classroom activities are broken up into two SEL categories, SELF and SOCIAL. Within each category there are two types of activities, Energizing/Warm Up and Focusing/Cool Down. Typically, the energizing activities include more movement and team-building, while the focusing activities include more mindfulness and breathwork, although some activities, like yoga, draw from multiple disciplines and include both movement and stillness at different points throughout the practice. (See the POP Chart diagram in Figure 2.4.)

These practices are designed for whole-class implementation (Tier 1), not for a few "problem students" to implement on their own or only with a social worker. Once the POP Chart is established, the activities become part of the morning check-in routine. The teacher may cue students who need help controlling their behavior to visit the POP Chart for a few minutes before returning to class, or the teacher may proactively insert a practice into the school day to help positively shift student energy towards being Ready to Learn. For students with exceptionalities, offer extended time in the POP Chart and include activity modifications to guarantee inclusivity. Guaranteeing an emotionally and physically safe and accessible environment is crucial for program implementation to be inclusive for all.

The activities are either written as "Extended Scripts," which include extensive classroom management cues and pacing suggestions, or are written as "Activities" (often as sequences), to be read aloud by the teacher or implemented as directed.

As I have mentioned in other areas of this book, I am not a fan of scripted material being the main delivery vehicle for practitioners, as it does not build teacher SEL competency or encourage reflection. The intention behind the design of the scripted activities below is to give the educator a vehicle in which to learn the delivery, pacing, and classroom management style that best complements the content. Given the length, the scripts are not designed to be read aloud to the students. Instead, it is recommended the teacher read through the scripts a few times to get a full picture of what the delivery looks, sounds, and feels like so that an emotionally and physically safe space is created for the instruction to take place. Once the practitioner has mastered the pacing and classroom management cues, the POP Chart becomes a living, functioning element of the teacher's classroom, meeting both student and teacher needs throughout the school day. As each classroom is different, one quadrant of the POP Chart may meet the needs of one particular classroom more than another. The materials in each quadrant, as well as in the corresponding Professional Development Facilitators' Guides, are scaffolded so that teachers can select the activities that best move their classrooms from Self-Awareness to Self-Regulation to Social Awareness through to finding the balance between Self-Efficacy and Social Harmony.

The activities are experiential in nature and empower students to read and respond proactively to their bodies' cues. The word "practice" is often used when framing the activities, as it also is in the morning check-in routine. It is important that the work is messaged to the students as something they practice, instead of something they do once and move on. By practicing the strategies again and again, the students are able to cultivate that duality between the mental and the physical or the body and the mind. As present in both the SELF and SOCIAL activities, the union between the mental and the physical is cultivated through four interconnected disciplines:

Vocalization: speaking, chanting, singing
Movement: gross/fine/locomotor, yoga, dance, fitness
Stillness: reflection, mindfulness, breathwork, meditation
Team-building: play, collaboration, communication

Most of these elements, such as voice, breath, stillness, and yoga, are interdisciplinary. For instance, stillness can be used to help cultivate an awareness of self while with others, or the personal within the interpersonal. Alternatively, movement can help one find focus through yoga or energy through a team-building activity. Ultimately, the goal is to utilize a mix of Mindful Practices to build Self-Awareness, Self-Regulation, and Social Awareness so that one can find the balance between Self-Efficacy and Social Harmony: the ability to maintain the needs of the self while in a social situation or, conversely, to balance the needs of the group with the needs of the self.

Using the Agreements and building consensus around the activity is important, not just to build an emotionally and physically safe environment, but also so that the teacher can gain feedback from the students on why they believe they are practicing this skill and what the goal of the activity is. Each lesson contains a cue to "Give the students the 'Why' of the activity," to help build student ownership of the material and to empower them with the SEL knowledge to find their words, name emotions, and be in control of their behavior.

For tips on how to reinforce the concepts of personal space and safe touch with your students, or additional implementation suggestions, please see the section on "Be the Solution: educator questions from the field" in the Appendix.

# 4

# SELF Activities:
# Warm Up and Energize

The activities in this chapter are written for kindergarten to fifth-grade classrooms. These activities are designed to be included in your classroom POP Chart in the "SELF: Warm Up and Energize" quadrant.

Although practiced in a group setting, these SELF: Warm Up and Energize activities are designed to engage students as individuals and positively shift their energy through yoga and movement.

After each activity has been taught, it should be added to the POP Chart, so that students can utilize it during their morning check-in routine, or if they need a break at any point throughout the day.

## Title: Brain Massage

**Extended Script ✓ Activity**

**Provide students with the "Why" of the activity:** Today, we are practicing **Brain Massage** so that we have a tool to use any time we are **anxious or worried and need to cool down**, focus, and Be In the Zone.

**Supplies:** Sentence strip to add the activity to the POP Chart

**Time:** 3 minutes

**Brain Massage** helps us focus and relax. I have already created a card for Brain Massage and added it to our POP Chart [Teacher points to card]. That way we can use our Brain Massage before a test, after recess, or any time our class needs to Be In the Zone and focus. This activity is a positive way to manage our emotions, and is also an easy thing to do if we are at home and need a break.

Brain Massage begins with a facial massage! Close your eyes and take a deep breath. Keeping your eyes closed and your breathing deep, tap your fingertips on your forehead [pause for 5 seconds], around your eyes [pause for 5 seconds], down your cheekbones [pause for 5 seconds], on the bridge of your nose [pause for 5 seconds], and on your chin [pause for 5 seconds].

Next, place your fingertips on top of your head and gently squeeze and massage around your head for the count of 10. [Teacher counts aloud to 10.]

Lastly, let's give ourselves a calming head massage. Place two fingers on your temples, or the side of your head. Move your fingers in circles for the count of 10 deep, relaxing breaths. [Teacher counts aloud to 10.]

Well done, Room [x]! Brain Massage is an important Social-Emotional Learning activity. It helps us remember to take the time to care for both our bodies and our minds, because the two work together to keep us healthy and Ready to Learn!

## Title: Yoga Sequence 1: (Seated Poses)

Seated Arm Stretch, Seated Twist, and Side Body Stretch

**Teacher Script ✓ Activity**

**Provide students with the "Why" of the activity:** Today, we are practicing yoga so that we can **focus, concentrate**, and be Ready to Learn. This activity also helps us stay healthy by giving us a movement break.

**Supplies:** Sentence strip to add the activity to the POP Chart

**Time:** 5 minutes [poses may be done in isolation or as a sequence]

I am going to lead us through **Yoga Sequence 1**. This first sequence is designed to be simple, relaxing, and fun! Yoga is a practice where we move our bodies into different shapes or poses. Yoga connects the body and mind through movement and breathing. If you ever feel like you are getting tired or that it is hard to breathe, simply pause for a moment and close your eyes. There is no good or bad way to practice yoga. The two most important things are that you try your best and listen to your body. Does anyone have any questions about yoga before we get started? [Teacher responds to student questions.]

Our first pose is **Seated Arm Stretch**. Hold the pose only as long as you are comfortable. Once you begin to get tired, release the pose and find your breath.

**First:** Begin seated, with your feet flat on the floor. Lift your arms to a "T" position.

**Then:** Raise your arms above your head, and interlace your fingers.

**Next:** Flip your palms to the ceiling, and move your shoulders down and away from your ears.

**Last:** Close your eyes, and take five deep, slow yoga breaths. Yoga breathing is when you pull a calm, relaxing breath from deep inside your body. When you are done, slowly lower your arms.

To transition to **Seated Twist**, students stay seated at their desks. Twists can be very good for letting go of any unwanted stress or negativity.

**First:** Inhale and lengthen your spine. Close your eyes and take in a deep, slow yoga breath. Take a moment to scan the body and the mind. Notice if there is anything negative that you would like to let go of. With a deep exhalation, release it now. [Teacher models deep exhalation.]

**Then:** Keeping your feet planted firmly on the ground, exhale and rotate your torso to the right side. Have your eyes find a spot over your right shoulder on which to focus. Take five deep, slow yoga breaths. On the last breath, come back to center.

**Next:** Keeping your feet planted firmly on the ground, inhale and lengthen your spine. Exhale and rotate your torso to the left side. Have your eyes find a spot over your left shoulder on which to focus. Take five deep, slow yoga breaths. On the last breath, come back to center.

**Last:** Close your eyes, and take five deep, slow yoga breaths. Try to clear your mind of absolutely everything. Simply notice the pattern of the breath moving in and out of your body. Don't try to change the rhythm of the breath, just follow it.

To transition to **Gentle Neck Stretch**, students stay seated at their desks. This yoga pose is an excellent solution if you feel stress in the neck or body and want to relax.

**First:** Inhale and lengthen your spine. Close your eyes and take in a deep, slow yoga breath.

**Then:** Sit so there is space between your back and the back of your chair. Lengthen your spine and place your left hand on your desk and your right fingertips on your right shoulder.

**Next:** Rotate your right elbow so it is in line with your shoulder. Breathing in, tilt your left ear towards your left shoulder. Maintain a square and still upper body while you use your right fingertips to apply light pressure on the right shoulder.

**Last:** Focus your gaze over your left shoulder. Take five deep, slow yoga breaths. If at any point you feel a pull, release the pose. When you are done, bring yourself back to a neutral position with a tall spine. Exhale and roll shoulders back three times.

[Repeat on the other side.]

## Title: Yoga Sequence 2

Starfish, Horse, and Seated Arm Stretch

**Extended Script ✓ Activity**

**Provide students with the "Why" of the activity:** Today, we are practicing yoga so that we can **focus, concentrate**, and be Ready to Learn. This activity also helps us stay healthy by getting us up and out of our seats to take a movement break.

**Supplies:** Sentence strip to add the activity to the POP Chart

**Time:** 7 minutes [poses may be done in isolation or as a sequence]

I am going to lead us through **Yoga Sequence 2**. Yoga is a practice where we move our bodies into different shapes or poses. Yoga connects the body and mind through movement and breathing. As we talked about last time, if you ever feel like you are getting tired or that it is hard to breathe, simply pause for a moment and close your eyes. There is no good or bad way to practice yoga. The two most important things are that you try your best and listen to your body. Does anyone have any questions about yoga before we get started? [Teacher responds to student questions.]

When I say "Begin," please stand up and push in your chairs. [Teacher cues students and they all stand and push in their chairs.] Please stay behind your desk, at least arms-width apart from your neighbor. It is important to keep our classroom safe by honoring our classmates' personal space.

★ **Teacher Tip:** For movement in the classroom to be successful, it is vital that you articulate, model, and reinforce the concept of personal space. For the physical and emotional safety of the classroom to be maintained, personal space should be taught and practiced in varying settings (i.e. lining up for dismissal, hallway behavior, lunchroom, recess, PE class, etc.) and by multiple stakeholders in the building all using common language around the concept. If a student's personal space is violated, you should pause the activity and reteach personal space before continuing with the lesson.

Our first pose is **Starfish Pose**. Hold the pose only as long as you are comfortable. Once you begin to get tired, release the pose and find your breath.

**First:** Begin by standing with your feet parallel, hip-width apart, arms in a horizontal "T" position. Step your feet out so your heels are below the midline of your forearms.

**Then:** Make sure your feet are parallel. Raise your arms above your head so your body makes an "X."

**Next:** Ground your shoulders down, and have energetic, high five hands.

**Last:** Extend energetically in all five directions (down into the floor through your feet, out through both hands, and up out of the crown of your head). Close your eyes, and take five deep, slow yoga breaths. Yoga breathing is when you pull calm, relaxing breath from deep within your body.

Nicely done! Now we are going to learn another yoga pose, **Horse**. Just as with Starfish Pose, only the hold the poses as long as you are comfortable. Once you begin to get tired, release the pose and find your breath.

**First:** Begin by standing with your feet parallel, hip-width apart. Separate your feet so your heels are below the midline of your forearms.

**Then:** Turn both feet out so your heels are in and your toes are out (moving in the direction of a 180-degree angle).

**Next:** Press your palms together with your fingers toward the sky.

**Last:** Bend your knees, and sink your torso down. Be sure to keep your spine long and tall. Close your eyes, and take five deep, slow yoga breaths.

[The teacher will now choose a student demonstrating Be the Solution behavior to lead the class through a quick pose review.] Let's take a moment to review these two poses we have learned. I am looking for a student with Be the Solution behavior to lead us through a review of the poses. [Teacher chooses student.] Let's all practice Starfish pose for five yoga breaths. [Teacher counts to 5, student model poses.] Nicely done, Room [x]. Now, let's all practice Horse pose for 5 yoga breaths. [Teacher counts to 5, student model poses.] Excellent work, everyone.

We will now close our yoga time with **Seated Arm Stretch**. For Seated Arm Stretch, we will need to return to our seats. Everyone, please place your feet flat on the floor and sit with a tall spine by the count of 5. [Teacher counts to 5. Students find seats.]

**First:** Begin in a seated position. Lift your arms to a "T" position.

**Then:** Raise your arms above your head, and interlace your fingers.

**Next:** Flip your palms to the ceiling, and ground your shoulders down.

**Last:** Close your eyes, and take five deep, slow yoga breaths. Remember, yoga breathing is when you pull a calm, relaxing breath from deep within your body.

Room [x], you all did an awesome job practicing yoga today. Well done! [Student name], you did a very nice job managing your behavior during the activity and respecting your neighbor's personal space. Can you please make cards for the three yoga poses we learned today? Can I have a volunteer to tell me the names of the three yoga poses we practiced together as a class? [Teacher calls on student. Student repeats poses.] That's right, [student name], we learned [teacher says names aloud while writing them on the board] Starfish Pose, Horse Pose, and Seated Arm Stretch. [Student name], will you please make cards for Starfish Pose, Horse Pose, and Seated Arm Stretch to add to our POP Chart? [Student walks to the center, writes the name of the poses each on a sentence strip, and adds them to the pocket chart.] Now, our class has another strategy to help us use our extra energy productively, so we can cool down, focus, and be Ready to Learn.

## Title: Yoga Sequence 3

Mountain Pose, Tippy Toes Breath, and Tree Pose

### Extended Script ✓ Activity

**Provide students with the "Why" of the activity:** Today, we are practicing Mountain Pose, Tippy Toes Breath, and Tree Pose. These are yoga and balancing poses that help us **focus on the present moment, clearing our minds of any stress or tension**. These activities also help us stay healthy by getting us up and out of our seats to take a movement break.

**Supplies:** Sentence strip to add the activity to the POP Chart

**Time:** 7 minutes [poses may be done in isolation or as a sequence]

I am going to lead us through **Yoga Sequence 3**. Yoga is a practice where we move our bodies into different shapes or poses. Yoga connects the body and mind through movement and breathing. Remember, if you ever feel like you are getting tired or that it is hard to breathe, simply pause for a moment and close your eyes. There is no good or bad way to practice yoga. The two most important things are that you try your best and listen to your body. Does anyone have any questions about yoga before we get started? [Teacher responds to student questions.]

When I say "Begin," please stand up and push in your chairs. [Teacher cues students and they all stand and push in their chairs.] Please stay behind your desk, at least arms-width apart from your neighbor. It is important to keep our classroom safe by honoring our classmates' personal space.

Our first pose is **Mountain Pose**. Hold the pose only as long as you are comfortable. Once you begin to get tired, release the pose and find your breath.

**First:** Plant your right foot onto the ground, and count, "One!" Plant your left foot onto the ground, and count, "Two!" Make sure your feet are parallel like train tracks.

**Then:** Shoot your right arm straight down next to your body, fingers actively pointing down, and count, "Three!" Do the same with your left arm, counting, "Four!"

**Next:** Extend the crown of your head to the ceiling to lengthen your whole spine, roll your shoulders back and settle your eyes on a focal point, counting, "Five!"

**Last:** Distribute your weight evenly between both feet as you stand tall and proud. Take five slow, deep yoga breaths.

To transition to **Tippy Toes Breath**, students stay standing next to their desks.

**First:** Stand next to your desk with a tall spine. As you get started, place a hand on your chair to help you balance.

**Then:** Focus your gaze on a point in front of you. Choose a spot that is not moving, such as a floor tile or desk leg.

**Next:** Stand on your tiptoes. Inhaling and staying on your tiptoes, bend your knees to lower yourself about 4 inches as you count to 4, keeping your back tall and upright. Inhaling and staying on your tiptoes, lower yourself 4 more inches as you count to four. Exhaling and staying on your tiptoes, rise back to standing as you count to 4.

**Last:** Let's hone our concentration skills and practice Tippy Toes Breath again together.

To transition to **Tree Pose**, students stay standing next to their desks.

**First:** Begin by standing with your feet parallel, no more than hip-width apart. Focus your gaze on a point in front of you.

**Then:** Shift your weight onto your right leg. Lift your left leg, and turn it out to the side while you keep your hips facing forward.

**Next:** Place your left foot above or below your right knee. Press your foot into your leg as the leg presses back into your foot.

**Last:** Lift your arms overhead like the branches of a tree. Repeat on the left side.

Students take their seats.

# 5

# SELF Activities:
# Cool Down and Focus

The activities in this chapter are written for kindergarten to fifth-grade classrooms, with modifications suggested for early childhood learners and students with exceptionalities. These activities are designed to be included in your classroom POP Chart in the "SELF: Cool Down and Focus" quadrant.

Although practiced in a group setting, these SELF: Cool Down and Focus activities are designed to engage students as individuals and positively shift their energy through relaxation, mindfulness, and reflection.

After each activity has been taught, it should be added to the POP Chart, so that students can utilize it during their morning check-in routine, or if they need a break at any point throughout the day.

## Title: Write and Rip

### ✓ Extended Script Activity

**Provide students with the "Why" of the activity:** Today, we are practicing **Write and Rip** to help us **release negative feelings** so that we are Ready to Learn. This is a great activity to practice at home if you are ever feeling stressed, sad, or worried.

**Supplies:** Sentence strip to add the activity to the POP Chart
Scratch paper
Recycling bin or garbage can
Clock or timer

**Time:** 5 minutes

Let's move on to today's Social-Emotional Learning activity, Write and Rip.

We are practicing Write and Rip because it helps us learn Self-Awareness and understand how emotions affect our mind and bodies. It gives us a strategy to let go of any tension or stress that may be bothering us physically or emotionally. To begin, pause for a moment, close your eyes, and scan your body. Notice if there is any part of your body where you may be holding stress, such as your shoulders or your stomach. Is there something stressful that is making your shoulders tight or your stomach hurt? Is there anything on your mind today that you need to let go of? Like something you are worried about or something that makes you sad?

We're going to practice Write and Rip by writing our negative thoughts and worries on a piece of scratch paper, then ripping them up and tossing them into the recycle bin. You have the length of one song during which to write. You may also draw, if it is easier for you to express your emotions by drawing. [Teacher moves recycling bin to the center of the room and demonstrates writing while the music plays, stops the music and rips up the page.] By ripping up and tossing our worries in the trash, this helps us let go of stress and negativity and helps us be in control of our emotions and Be Ready to Learn. Please know that no one will see what you write, even me. You may write in English, Spanish, Polish, or any language in which you feel comfortable expressing yourself. All pages are ripped up and put in the recycle bin.

Before we begin, I need to find a student who is demonstrating Be the Solution behavior by sitting up tall, with two feet flat on the floor, hands folded and respecting their neighbor's personal space, who can restate the activity in her own words.

[Teacher calls on student demonstrating the expectations. Student restates activity.]

Thank you, [student name]. Room [x], do we see any potential problems with implementing this activity? [Teacher calls on one or two students to discuss potential pitfalls.]

Thank you, [student names]. So, now that we know where the problems may occur, how can we Be the Solution? What Agreements do we need to make for the activity to be physically and emotionally safe for all? What are the consequences if the Agreements are broken?

> ★ **Teacher Tip:** For this consensus-building strategy to be successful, it is imperative that you consistently uphold the Agreements and enforce the consequences, if the Agreements are broken, to maintain an emotionally and physically safe classroom environment.

We have time for [x number of] students to share their thoughts. Before we share, let's remember to listen intently to others, accept others' opinions and be careful not to interrupt our classmates.

[Teacher calls on students and writes the Agreements and consequences on the board. This is also the perfect time for the teacher to suggest modifications to the activity for students with limited physical mobility, students with self-esteem challenges, students who are deaf and hard of hearing, English language learners, and students with exceptionalities.]

Thank you, [student names]. Now that we have our Agreements and consequences on the board, let's Check for Understanding. Please raise your right hand in the air. A "high five" hand tells me you understand the activity, our Agreements, and the consequences if the Agreements are broken, and you are all set to begin. Two fingers in the air, or a peace sign, tells me that you have a question or comment that needs to be addressed before we begin. A fist in the air tells me that you are unsure and you are not ready to begin, which is OK. It is important that we have created a physically and emotionally safe classroom environment for our activity to take place.

[Teacher observes the room and responds appropriately to student needs by answering questions, restating activity, building consensus, etc.]

Thank you, Room [x], for sharing your thoughts respectfully and thoughtfully. I witnessed students actively listening to their peers. Well done! Now, please get out your pencils and a piece of scratch paper. Once we are done ripping up our papers, I will place the recycle bin behind my desk, so that you are reassured that the contents of the bin will not be tampered with. When I say "Begin" I will turn on the music. You will have the length of one song to write or draw any negative emotions or worries you may have. When the song is over, we will all rip up our papers and toss them in the recycle bin.

[Teacher makes sure every student has scratch paper and a writing utensil. Teacher begins music and the students begin to write. It is recommended that the teacher also participates in the activity to model appropriate strategies for dealing with stress and anxiety. When the song concludes, the teacher stops the music and asks all the students to rip up their pages. Teacher prompts the students row by row to walk up to the recycling bin to toss their pages. Once the last row is done, it is nice if the teacher can place the recycle bin behind her desk, or tie off the garbage bag, so that the students are reassured that the contents of the bin will not be tampered with.]

Great job, Room [x]! I am impressed with your behavioral choices. I witnessed students developing emotional awareness and learning a new way to let go of negative emotions. I witnessed students Self-Regulating and making positive decisions about their behavior. I also witnessed students honoring the Agreements. Thank you!

[Student name], you did an excellent job managing your behavior during the activity and respecting your neighbor's personal space. Can you please create a card for Write and Rip to add to our POP Chart? [Student walks to POP Chart, writes the name of the activity on a sentence strip, and adds it to the pocket chart.]

That way, our class has another strategy to help us be Ready to Learn any time we need to let go of negative thoughts or feelings. Remember, Room [x], we can also practice Write and Rip at home, any time we feel stress in our bodies or our minds.

While [student name] is adding Write and Rip to our POP Chart, we have time for [x number of] students to share their emotions and feelings with a one-word check-in.

Again, I am looking for students who are sitting up tall, with two feet flat on the floor, hands folded, and respecting their neighbor's personal space, who can share one word with our class. [Teacher calls on students to share one word such as "Relaxed" or "Calm."]

## Title: Still Point

**Extended Script ✓ Activity**

**Provide students with the "Why" of the activity:** Today, we are practicing Still Point. This activity is a great way to **relax when we are feeling worried**. This activity has two parts. The first part is to help us find a calm, relaxed state. The second is to create a simple way for us to find that relaxed state or Still Point, any time we are stressed or worried.

**Supplies:** Sentence strip to add the activity to the POP Chart

**Time:** 2 minutes

**First:** We are going to find a cooling, relaxing breath by curling our tongues and sipping air through them, like a straw. Let's all inhale now to the count of 3 [teacher models inhalation] and exhale through our noses to the count of 3 [teacher models exhalation].

**Then:** We are going to find this cooling breath again. This time, when we are breathing and feeling relaxed, we are going to cross our middle and index fingers together [teacher demonstrates]. Let's practice this together, inhaling through our "straw" to the count of 3 [teacher models inhalation] and exhaling through our noses to the count of 3 [teacher models exhalation]. Now that we are relaxed, calm, and have found our **Still Point**, let's cross our fingers [teacher demonstrates].

**Next:** We are going to practice this strategy again. By finding a relaxing state and crossing our fingers, we are training our bodies to find that peaceful, relaxed state – or **Still Point** – every time our fingers are crossed.

Let's practice it again! Inhaling through our "straw" to the count of 3 [teacher models inhalation] and exhaling through our noses to the count of 3 [teacher models exhalation]. Now that we are relaxed, calm, and have found our Still Point, let's cross our fingers [teacher demonstrates].

**Last:** I need to find students who are demonstrating our Be the Solution behavior by sitting up tall, with two feet flat on the floor, hands folded, and respecting their neighbor's personal space, who can share examples of different times they could use this strategy throughout the day. We have time for [x number of] students to share their thoughts. Before we share, let's remember to listen intently to others, accept others' opinions, and be careful not to interrupt our classmates. [Teacher calls on students demonstrating the expectations. Teacher writes examples on board.]

Thank you, [student names]. Room [x], are there any other times, maybe at home, when you are taking a test, during recess or over the weekend, when this strategy would also be useful? How can you find your Still Point in other tough situations? [Teacher calls on an additional one or two students to share and writes their ideas on the board.]

Thank you, [student names]. So, now that we know when stressful situations may occur, we can Be the Solution and find our Still Points so we can remain cool, relaxed and focused.

★ **Teacher Tip:** Continue to practice Still Point throughout the day to reinforce and model the concept for your students. Remind students to "find their Still Points" if they encounter a tough situation in the playground or find themselves dealing with stress and anxiety at home. This activity is great for state testing, but should be practiced well before then, to give the students a solid foundation for implementation.

## Title: Lion's Breath

### ✓ Extended Script Activity

**Provide students with the "Why" of the activity:** Today, we are practicing **Lion's Breath** to help us **release any anger or sadness** that we may be experiencing so that we can Be the Solution and be Ready to Learn.

**Supplies:** Sentence strip to add the activity to the POP Chart

**Time:** 2 minutes

We are practicing Lion's Breath today because it helps us learn Self-Awareness and understand how emotions affect our bodies. It gives us a strategy to let go of any tension or stress that is held in our bodies. Pause for a moment, close your eyes, and scan your body. Notice if there is any part of your body where you may be holding stress, such as your shoulders or your stomach. Is there a part of your body that feels tight or achy? Perhaps you notice that your stomach hurts or you get headaches when you feel nervous, anxious, or stressed? When we practice Lion's Breath, we breathe calming, cooling breaths to the parts of our bodies that most need to relax.

We are going to breathe like lions by inhaling and exhaling strongly and deeply [teacher demonstrates]. Sometimes, being strong is taking a moment to stop and listen to your body. Letting go helps us focus and find our center, so we can be in control of our bodies and our emotions.

Before we begin, I need to find a student who is demonstrating our Be the Solution behavior by sitting up tall, with two feet flat on the floor, hands folded, and respecting their neighbor's personal space, who can restate the activity in their own words. [Teacher calls on student demonstrating the expectations. Student restates activity.]

Thank you, [student name]. Room [x], do we see any potential problems with implementing this activity? [Teacher calls on one or two students to discuss potential pitfalls.]

Thank you, [student names]. So, now that we know where the problems may occur, how can we Be the Solution? What Agreements do we need to make for the activity to be physically and emotionally safe for all? What are the consequences if the Agreements are broken?

★ **Teacher Tip:** For this consensus-building strategy to be successful, it is imperative that you consistently uphold the Agreements and enforce the consequences. If class members violate the Agreements, then the consequences must be implemented, or else the students will no longer trust that the classroom environment is safe.

We have time for [x number of] students to share their thoughts. Before we share, let's remember to listen intently to others, accept others' opinions, and be careful not to interrupt our classmates.

[Teacher calls on students and writes the Agreements and consequences on the board. This is also the perfect time for the teacher to suggest modifications to the activity for students with limited physical mobility, students with self-esteem challenges, students who are deaf and hard of hearing, English language learners, or students with exceptionalities.]

Thank you, [student names]. Now that we have our Agreements and consequences on the board, let's Check for Understanding. Please raise your right hand in the air. A "high five" hand tells me you understand the activity, our Agreements, and the consequences if the Agreements are broken, and you are all set to begin. Two fingers in the air, or a peace sign, tells me that you have a question or comment that needs to be addressed before we begin. A fist in the air tells me that you are unsure and you are not ready to begin, which is OK. It is important that we have created a physically and emotionally safe classroom environment for our activity to take place.

[Teacher reads room and responds appropriately to student needs by answering questions, restating activity, building consensus, etc.]

Thank you, Room [x], for sharing your thoughts respectfully and thoughtfully. I witnessed students actively listening to their peers. Well done! Now, let's begin Lion's Breath!

**First:** Sit at your desk with your feet flat on the floor. Close your eyes, and lay your hands flat on your desk, palms down. Roll your shoulders back and sit up tall.

**Then:** Place two fingers at the top of your jaw, close to your ears.

**Next:** Take a deep breath. Breathing out to the count of four, open your mouth wide as you draw fingers down to your chin.

★ **Teacher Tip:** students should not "roar" or be verbal at this time. For some students who may have experienced trauma, sitting with their eyes closed can feel unsafe, so provide them with the option of turning their bodies so they are not facing another student or sitting with their backs up against the wall.

**Last:** Let's keep our eyes closed and repeat Lion's Breath four more times together. As you exhale, release any stress or tension that you are holding in your body.

Well done, Room [x]. I am impressed with your behavioral choices. I witnessed students developing emotional and body awareness. I witnessed students making positive decisions about their behavior and I witnessed students honoring our Agreements. Thank you!

[Student name], you did an excellent job managing your behavior during the activity and respecting your neighbor's personal space. Can you please create a card for Lion's Breath to add to our POP Chart? [Student walks to center, writes the name of the activity on a sentence strip, and adds it to the pocket chart.]

That way, our class has another strategy to help us be Ready to Learn any time we are stressed or anxious. Remember, Room [x], we can also practice Lion's Breath at home, any time we feel stress in our bodies.

While [student name] is adding Lion's Breath to our POP Chart, we have time for [x number of] students to share their emotions and feelings with a one-word check-in.

Again, I am looking for students who are sitting up tall, with two feet flat on the floor, hands folded, and respecting their neighbor's personal space, who can share one word with our class. [Teacher calls on students to share one word such as "Relaxed" or "Calm."]

## Title: Ready to Learn Breath

**Teacher Script ✓ Activity**

**Provide students with the "Why" of the activity:** Today, we are practicing **Ready to Learn** Breath. We can use Ready to Learn Breath when we are feeling overwhelmed or upset, or any time our class needs to Be In the Zone and focus. This activity is a **positive way to check in, focus,** and get our minds Ready to Learn.

**Supplies:** Sentence strip to add the activity to the POP Chart
Notebook or scratch paper
Pens and pencils
Clock or timer

**Time:** 3 minutes

**First:** Close your eyes and focus on your breath. Just follow your breath as it moves in and out. Try not to change the speed or rhythm of your breath. Leave it just as it is. As you continue to breathe, notice if you feel anything in your body. If you do, don't worry about changing it. Just notice what you are feeling and breathe in and breathe out.

There is no right way or wrong way. Just breathe.

**Then:** Listen for a sound far away. Choose one sound outside of your classroom to focus on. Focus all of your attention on that sound. Breathe it in, and breathe it out for the next five breaths [teacher softly counts to 5].

**Next:** Leave that noise behind and focus your attention on a sound that is closer to you. A noise inside the classroom, such as the buzz of a computer or the hum of an overhead light. Listen only to one sound, nothing else. Breathe it in, and breathe it out for the next five breaths [teacher softly counts to 5].

**Last:** Leave both sounds behind and focus only on the soft, quiet sound of your own breathing. For the next five breaths observe only the sound of your breathing, tune out everything else [teacher softly counts to 5].

Now clear your mind. Before you open your eyes, check in with how you are feeling. Has your breath changed? What do you need to do to be Ready to Learn for the rest of the school day? Before we move on, repeat this statement three times in your mind, "I give myself permission not to be perfect. The most important thing is that I try my best." [Teacher repeats statement softly three times.]

Finally, as we close our Ready to Learn Breath today, picture yourself being focused, relaxed, and Ready to Learn.

In the next three breaths, open your eyes. Identify three items that look familiar, such as a chair, a pencil, or a book. Once you have found your three items, sit with your hands folded and your eyes on me, your teacher. This formally concludes our Ready to Learn Breath. However, we can decide as a class to use this strategy any time throughout the week when we need help self-regulating, working as a team, or focusing for a test. We will now transition to [x] activity.

## Title: Equal Breath

**Extended Script ✓ Activity**

**Provide students with the "Why" of the activity:** Today, we are practicing **Equal Breath**. We can use Equal Breath when we are feeling **confused, hyper, or upset**. This activity is a positive way to check in, focus, and prepare our minds to be Ready to Learn.

**Supplies:** Sentence strip to add the activity to the POP Chart

**Time:** 3 minutes

**First:** Begin seated and place your feet flat on the floor, roll your shoulders back and lengthen your spine.

**Then:** Notice the pattern of your natural breath. Notice the inhalations and the exhalations. Which is longer? Which is deeper?

**Next:** With your next breath, make your inhalation and exhalation the same length. Let's start with the count of 4. Slowly count to 4 as you inhale. [Teacher slowly counts aloud] 1 – 2 – 3 – 4. Now, also count to 4 as you exhale. The exercise is to match the length of your inhalation and exhalation.

**Last:** Continue breathing this way for several minutes. You may experiment with changing the number you count to, just make sure your inhalation and exhalation stay the same length.

★ **Teacher Tip:** For early childhood students, visibly count along on your fingers to help them keep the pace of the activity.

## Title: Name It and Doodle It!

**Extended Script ✓ Activity**

**Provide students with the "Why" of the activity:** Today, we are practicing **Name It and Doodle It!** This activity **helps us identify, name, and understand our emotions**. This is a great activity to practice at home if we feel overwhelmed, sad, or worried.

**Supplies:** Sentence strip to add the activity to the POP Chart
Notebook or scratch paper
Pens, pencils, and/or crayons
Clock or timer

**Time:** 5 minutes

**First:** The teacher reads the feelings and emotions *Happy, Relaxed, Energetic, Excited, Tired, Bored, Worried, Vulnerable, Hungry, Sad, Scared,* and *Angry* listed on the POP Chart.

**Then:** The teacher cues the students: "Close your eyes and take three deep breaths. Notice what you are feeling in your body. Notice what thoughts are in your mind. [Teacher waits while students take three breaths.] Open your eyes and write down a feeling or emotion that you are experiencing. It can be one from the POP Chart, or one that is not listed. There is no correct or incorrect feeling or emotion for this activity."

**Next:** The teacher instructs the students: "For the next 4 minutes you are going to doodle, write, or draw something that expresses what you are feeling. There is no right or wrong way to complete your story or picture. The only requirement is that you write or draw for the entire 4 minutes. Get your pencils ready – take a breath – and begin!" [Teacher sets the timer for 4 minutes and writes "Start Time: and Stop Time:" on the board.]

**Last:** The teacher stops the timer and asks students to put their pencils down. The teacher asks the students to take five breaths and examine what they doodled. The teacher then cues the students to: "Notice what you are feeling in the body and in the mind. Do you feel any different after you took time to name and doodle what you are experiencing in the body and mind? Can you think of times when stopping to name and doodle your feelings and emotions might help you feel in control or make positive choices about your behavior?"

★ **Teacher Tip:** Think of where you would like your students to store their drawings. Perhaps they keep all their drawings in a notebook, folder, or binder? If time permits, you can also ask the students to share their drawings with a partner. This is a great way to facilitate peer-to-peer communication and to help students manage vulnerability. This activity fuses perfectly with the POP Chart Check-In that is part of the morning routine. It is also a great solution for students who finish their work early or are easily distracted and need a positive way to channel their energy. For early childhood learners or students with exceptionalities who are not writing fluently, provide the option to color with crayons or to sculpt their feelings and emotions with molding clay. If time permits, teachers and aides can circulate the classroom and help students label items in their drawings and record keywords.

## Title: Secret Note

**Extended Script ✓ Activity**

**Provide students with the "Why" of the activity:** Today, we are writing ourselves a **Secret Note**. This activity is a creative way to **support ourselves in a challenging situation** when we are feeling sad or scared.

**Supplies:** Sentence strip to add the activity to the POP Chart
Notebook or scratch paper
Pens, pencils, and/or crayons

**Time:** 2 minutes

**First:** Students obtain a small sheet of scratch paper and a pencil.

**Then:** Before they begin writing, they find their breath and check in. What do they need to remember to be strong in a tough situation today?

**Next:** The students write themselves a note to keep with them throughout the day. The note can be a confidence boost or a gentle reminder. The note can read, "I will do a great job on my math test," or "I will not get into a fight on the playground today."

**Last:** Cue the students to take out their note when they need a quick boost.

★ **Teacher Tip:** This activity is great for students that go home to challenging domestic situations. To ensure privacy and anonymity, have the students refrain from putting their names or other's names on their notes, just in case they are misplaced. If students passing notes in your classroom is a problem, pass out index cards or colored paper to differentiate this note from others that may be circulating in your room. For early childhood learners or students with exceptionalities who are not writing fluently, provide the option to color with crayons. If time permits, teachers and aides can circulate the classroom and help students label items in their drawings and record keywords.

## Title: Memory Minute

**Extended Script ✓ Activity**

**Provide students with the "Why" of the activity:** Today, we will be practicing **Memory Minute** to help us **cool down and focus** when we are taking a test or having a difficult time remembering information. Memory Minute helps us release stress so that we can focus and Be In the Zone.

**Supplies:** Sentence strip to add the activity to the POP Chart
Clock or timer

**Time:** 2 minutes

**First:** Make sure your room is quiet and that all screens are turned off or not visible. Instruct the students to show you Be the Solution behavior by siting up tall, with their feet flat on the floor, and their hands folded on their desks. Cue the students to roll their shoulders back three times, respecting their neighbor's personal space.

**Then:** Instruct the students to visualize a blank sheet of paper and to clear their minds of all thoughts.

**Next:** Set the timer for 1 minute, and instruct the students to remain quiet. Tap a chime or softly clap twice to signal the beginning of Memory Minute. For 1 minute everyone, including the teacher, is quiet and focused.

**Last:** At the end of the minute, tap a chime or softly clap twice to signal the ending of Memory Minute.

★ **Teacher Tip:** For early childhood students, begin practicing Memory Minute for 30 seconds and increase the time in small increments of 5 seconds throughout the year.

# 6

# SOCIAL Activities:
# Warm Up and Energize

The activities in this chapter are written for kindergarten to fifth-grade classrooms, with modifications suggested throughout for early childhood learners and students with exceptionalities. These activities are designed to be included in your classroom POP Chart in the "SOCIAL: Warm Up and Energize" quadrant.

As they are practiced in a group setting, these SOCIAL: Warm Up and Energize activities are designed to engage students interpersonally and positively harness their energy through movement and teamwork.

After each activity has been taught, it should be added to the POP Chart, so you can utilize it any time throughout the day when your class needs to focus and get In the Zone.

## Title: Cooperation Circle

### ✓ Extended Script Activity

**Provide students with the "Why" of the activity:** Today, we are practicing **Cooperation Circle** to develop our leadership, **peer-to-peer communication, and community-building skills**. Additionally, this activity also helps us stay healthy by getting us up and out of our seats to take a movement break.

**Supplies:** Sentence strip to add the activity to the POP Chart
Music
Scratch paper and pencils

**Time:** 10 minutes

**Cooperation Circle** is a Social-Emotional Learning activity that focuses how we work as a team toward a common goal. To practice Cooperation Circle, we are going to organize ourselves in a circle according to our birthdays *without talking*. When I say "Begin" we will have the length of one song to organize ourselves in a circle, according to our birthdays. You may use scratch paper or use your fingers to indicate the month and day of your birthday. Our circle will start here with January [teacher points to spot]. For birthdays with high numbers, like 15, stomp once for 10 or twice for 20. So, if Maggie's birthday is June 12th, she will hold up 6 fingers to find other students with June birthdays. Then she will stomp once and hold up 2 fingers to find her exact spot in the circle. Remember, we cannot talk!

Before we begin, I need to find a student who is demonstrating our Be the Solution behavior by sitting up tall, with two feet flat on the floor, hands folded, and respecting her neighbor's personal space, who can restate the activity in her own words. [Teacher calls on student demonstrating the expectations. Student restates activity.]

Thank you, [student name]. Room [x], do we see any potential problems with implementing this activity? [Teacher calls a student to discuss potential pitfalls.]

Thank you, [student names]. So, now that we know where the problems may occur, how can we Be the Solution? What Agreements do we need to make for the activity to be physically and emotionally safe for all? What are the consequences if the Agreements are broken?

★ **Teacher Tip:** For this consensus-building strategy to be successful, it is imperative that you consistently uphold the Agreements and enforce the consequences. If class members violate the Agreements, then the consequences must be implemented, or else the students will no longer trust that the classroom environment is safe.

We have time for [x number of] students to share their thoughts. Before we share, let's remember to listen intently to others, accept others' opinions, and be careful not to interrupt our classmates.

[Teacher calls on students and writes the Agreements and consequences on the board. This is also the perfect time for the teacher to suggest modifications to the activity for students with limited physical mobility, students with self-esteem challenges, students who are deaf and hard of hearing, English language learners, or children with exceptionalities.]

Thank you, [student names]. Now that we have our Agreements and consequences on the board, let's Check for Understanding. Please raise your right hand in the air. A "high five" hand tells me you understand the activity, our Agreements, and the consequences if the Agreements are broken, and you are all set to begin. Two fingers in the air, or a peace sign, tells me that you have a question or comment that needs to be addressed before we begin. A fist in the air tells me that you are unsure and you are not ready to begin, which is OK. It is important that we have created a physically and emotionally safe classroom environment for our activity to take place.

[Teacher observes room and responds appropriately to student needs by answering questions, restating activity, building consensus, etc.]

Thank you, Room [x], for sharing your thoughts respectfully and thoughtfully. I witnessed students actively listening to their peers and Being the Solution. Well done! Now, let's get ready to start our SEL activity for today, Cooperation Circle! Let's remember to practice our communication skills, such as making eye contact.

Please take out your scratch paper and pencils and write down your name and birthday. When I say "Begin" I will start the music and you will stand up and form your circle. Remember, at the end of the song, your Birthday Circle must be complete. [Teacher cues the students. Students stand up and form their circle.

The teacher does not intervene or help the students meet the goal. The teacher's responsibilities are only to be timekeeper by starting/stopping the music and to maintain a safe space by making sure that the Agreements are being upheld. If the students do not meet their goal in time, the teacher can restart the music. This is also a great time for the teacher to positively reinforce the Call to Action and recognize students who are Being the Solution or who are focused and In the Zone.]

Well done, Room [x]. I am impressed with your behavioral choices. I witnessed students working as a team. I witnessed students using appropriate communication and eye contact. And I witnessed students honoring our Agreements and Being the Solution. Thank you!

There are many ways we can organize ourselves into a circle for this activity. Today, we practiced organizing ourselves by birthday. Next time, we can practice organizing alphabetically by first or last names or numerically by shoe size or by the answer to different math problems. [Student name], you did an excellent job managing your behavior during the activity and Being the Solution. Can you please create a card for Cooperation Circle to add to our POP Chart? [Student walks to POP Chart, writes the name of the activity on a sentence strip, and adds it to the pocket chart.] That way, our class has another strategy to help us be Ready to Learn any time we are stressed or anxious.

> ★ **Teacher Tip:** For early childhood learners or students with exceptionalities, distribute cards with numbers or letters of the alphabet and have students organize themselves in order. Additional variations include colors, seasons, or shapes. Help orient the students to the activity by designating where the circle begins and ends: "The alphabet begins with the letter A and so the student with the letter A on his card should stand here on the rug."

## Title: Tap-In and Tap-Out

✓ **Extended Script Activity**

**Provide students with the "Why" of the activity:** Today, we are practicing **Tap-In and Tap-Out** to continue to **develop our leadership and community-building skills**. This activity also helps us stay healthy by getting us up and out of our seats to take a movement break.

**Supplies:** Sentence strip to add the activity to the POP Chart

**Time:** 5 minutes

When I say "Begin," please stand up and push in your chairs. [Teacher cues students and they all stand and push in their chairs.] Please stay behind your desk, at least arms-width apart from your neighbor. It is important to keep our classroom safe by honoring our classmates' personal space.

★ **Teacher Tip:** For movement in the classroom to be successful, it is vital that you articulate, model, and reinforce the concept of personal space. For the physical and emotional safety of the classroom to be maintained, personal space should be taught and practiced in varying settings (i.e. during movement activities, lining up for dismissal, hallway behavior, lunchroom, recess, PE class, etc.) and by multiple stakeholders in the building all using common language around the concept. If a student's personal space is violated, you should pause the activity and reteach personal space before continuing with the lesson. (For more information on teaching personal space, please see the section on "Be the Solution: educator questions from the field" in the Appendix.)

Our movement activity today is called Tap-In and Tap-Out. Please follow along with me, doing what I do. For instance, if I do jumping jacks for the count of 8, then you will do jumping jacks for the count of 8. If I freeze in mountain pose (standing pose) for the count of 8, then you will freeze in mountain pose for the count of 8. After my turn, I will look for a student with Be the Solution behavior to come forward and become the leader. I will walk over to that student and "tap" him on the shoulder, and he will take my place. Then, that student will lead for 8 counts or breaths, until he walks over and "taps" another student to come forward and take his place. We have time for four student leaders today. Before we get started, let's write sample movements on the board that would work for this activity.

★ **Teacher Tip:** Using student prompts, write down such activities as jumping jacks, running in place, squats, side stretches, lunges, hopping up and down, yoga poses, culturally relevant dances such as cumbia, salsa, stepping or line dancing, or mimicking sport movements such as dribbling, throwing/catching, swimming, or jumping rope. Writing activities on the board is critical for maintaining the flow of the activity, as students often get nervous and have a difficult time thinking of a movement once they are chosen to lead. If energy is low, play music to help get students energized and Ready to Learn. If energy is high, close with calming music to help slow down the tempo of the activity and help students find their center and get In the Zone.

As with all our movement activities, if any part of this activity is uncomfortable at any time, just stop and find your breath. It is your responsibility to always listen to your body and trust its cues.

All right, Room [x], let's get started! [The teacher starts a movement and the students follow along. Movements are broken into 8 counts or breaths. The teacher should move slowly, so the students have a chance to acclimate to the activity. After the teacher has lead for 8 breaths, he should choose a student demonstrating Be the Solution behavior to lead the class through the next round.] I see students respecting their neighbor's personal space. Nice work, Room [x]!

I am looking for a student with Be the Solution behavior to lead us through the next round. [Teacher chooses student, and that student comes to the front of the room, names a movement, and leads class through 8 counts of the movement.] Excellent work, [student name]! Now, you choose a classmate that is demonstrating Be the Solution behavior to lead us through the next round. [Student walks over and taps a classmate on the shoulder, and that student comes to the front of the room, names a movement, and leads the sequence. This continues until four students have had a turn. Teacher stops music to close the activity.]

Great job, [student name]! I am impressed with how our class respected our neighbor's personal space and stayed In the Zone during the activity. [Student name], you did a great job making positive choices about your behavior during the activity. Can you please make a card for Tap-In and Tap-Out and add it to our POP Chart? [Student walks to the center, writes the name of the activity on a sentence strip and adds it to the pocket chart.] Now, our class has a new movement activity to help us be aware of and work with our energy levels, so that we can cool down, focus, and be Ready to Learn.

## Title: Pass the Squeeze Circle and One-Word Check-In

**Extended Script ✓ Activity**

**Provide students with the "Why" of the activity:** Today, we are practicing **Pass the Squeeze Circle** to help us develop an **awareness of our classmates and ourselves**. This activity also helps us stay healthy by getting us up and out of our seats to take a movement break.

**Supplies:** Sentence strip to add the activity to the POP Chart

**Time:** 5 minutes

**First:** Organize your students in a circle. (Cooperation Circle is a great lead-in activity to this one!) Cue the students to look around the room and make eye contact with their classmates. Ask them to "Notice who is in the room with you and appreciate their special skills and talents. Now, take a breath and remember all the unique and special talents that YOU bring to this class as well."

Ask the students to close their eyes and stand together for 30 seconds of silent reflection, before beginning the next phase of the activity.

**Then:** Find a student that is demonstrating Be the Solution behavior to act as Circle Captain for the activity. She will open and close the **one-word check-in**, which allows you, as the teacher, to step in and participate once the directions have been given.

**Next:** Choose the cue below that is most relevant to your students' lives. Beginning with the Circle Captain, ask the class to say one word that _____ (see samples below). Before cueing the students, reflect on class happenings of the week. (Did state testing begin this week? Was there a gang shooting in the community? Is your class working hard to prepare for the school's winter music program? Was there an incident on the bus after school yesterday that needs to be addressed?)

Describes what you appreciate about your classmates.
Describes who you are.
Describes a time when you helped another student.
Describes how you are feeling right now.
Describes an example of when you were a good leader.
Describes an example of when you were a good listener.

Describes something of which you are proud.
Describes something that makes you happy.
Describes a time you kept your cool in a tough situation.
Describes a time something that makes you feel good about who you are.
Describes an example of teamwork you have seen in this class the past week.
Describes what keeps you from giving up when things get hard.
Describes how you stay motivated when you fail and don't succeed.
Describes how to relax, calm down, and get focused when you are stressed.
Describes what you appreciate about our classroom community.
Describes what being "Ready to Learn" means to you.
Describes something that motivates you to "Be the Solution."
Describes what being responsible means to you.
Describes something terrific about yourself.

Once each student has said her word, ask all the students to hold hands.

Beginning with the Circle Captain, she will silently Pass a Squeeze around the circle: she will squeeze the hand of the person to her right, then that person squeezes the hand of the person to his right, and so on, until the squeeze has made its way all the way around the circle. This activity may be done with eyes open or closed, but it must be silent. Once the squeeze has made its way back to the Circle Captain, she will say "Thank you," which will formally close the circle, and students will return to their seats.

★ **Teacher Tip:** If there is awkwardness or bickering when asking students to hold hands, simply say, "Left hand up, right hand down." To bring a joyous feel to the circle, have students make eye contact and "Pass a Laugh" instead of a squeeze. Laughter is contagious and can bring joy and happiness to any collaborative setting! If there is not time to have students form a circle, simply have them stand up at their desks to speak. Write the prompt on the board and give the students 1 minute of silence to reflect before they begin sharing with the group. For early childhood students, inform them it is OK to repeat another student's word. Also, softly count to three when it is each student's time to share a word, to help keep the pacing of the activity on track.

## Title: Pass the Clap Circle*

### Extended Script ✓ Activity

**Provide students with the "Why" of the activity:** Today, we are practicing **Pass the Clap** to give us an opportunity to **focus, collaborate, and work as a team**. This activity also helps us stay healthy by getting us up and out of our seats to take a movement break.

**Supplies:** Sentence strip to add the activity to the POP Chart

**Time:** 7 minutes

**First:** Arrange your students in one large circle, about arms-width apart, respecting their neighbor's personal space. Before beginning, invite all students to sit (or stand) with a tall back, eyes closed. Ask the students to spend the next 15 seconds following the rhythm of their breath, just checking in with where they are in space and time. What do they feel in their bodies? What thoughts are popping to mind?

**Then:** When the 15 seconds has concluded, choose a student to be Circle Captain and ask him to begin the activity by turning to the student to his left, making eye contact, and clapping at the same time.

**Next:** The student who received the clap now turns to the student on their left, makes eye contact and claps. This continues until each student in the circle is contributing. The clap moves quickly around the circle, with all eyes following the clap.

**Last:** After the clap has successfully made it around the circle once, then the Circle Captain should add another clap. [It is best if these claps are spaced equidistant around the circle.] Once both claps have made their way around the circle three times, then the Circle Captain closes the circle with "1–2–3– Stop."

Teacher Tips: Modify this activity to learn students' names at the beginning of the school year by moving around the circle saying the name of the student that receives the clap. For instance, the student on my right passes me the clap, so the whole group says "Carla." Then, I pass the clap to the student on my left and the whole group says, "Dottie," then on to "Penny," etc. This is a fantastic way to not only learn students' names but also to learn how to pronounce them correctly. For early childhood learners or students with exceptionalities, begin by passing a stuffed animal or a "paddy cake clap," making the eye contact optional for those students who find it inaccessible.

* Adapted from Viola Spolin's Pass the Clap.

## Title: Goal Setting Postcard

**Extended Script ✓ Activity**

**Provide students with the "Why" of the activity:** Today, we are creating **Goal Setting Postcards** to help us be **personally responsible and accountable**. This activity is great for reminding us that we can Be the Solution in our own lives when we feel frustrated or are facing a challenging task.

**Supplies:** Sentence strip to add the activity to the POP Chart
4 × 5 index cards, lined on one side
Pen or pencil

**Time:** 7 minutes

**First:** Write the following template on the board for the students to copy.

"In the next two weeks I will _____ [action verb] at _____ [time/day] because _____ [reason for action].

My classmate _____ [name of peer] will help me reach my goal, if I need support.

One bad habit or problem I will need to watch out for is _____ [potential problem]. I can Be the Solution by _____ [action verb].

Signed: _____ Date: _____

Witnessed: _____ Date: _____

**Then:** On the front of the index card (the side with lines), ask the students to copy the template and find a Thought Partner to complete their goal with them.

**Next:** On the back of the index card (the side without lines), ask the students to draw a picture of themselves "Being the Solution" and completing their goal.

**Last:** Once their Goal Setting Postcards are complete, ask the students to review what they have written and drawn. Then, ask them to sit up tall and close their eyes. For 1 minute, ask the students to visualize what it would look, feel, and sound like to meet their goal. Ask them to visualize themselves "Being the Solution" and reaching their goal. Once the minute concludes, ask for a few students to give you a one-word check-in, sharing one word about their goal.

★ **Teacher Tip:** This activity is ideal for students who need help setting behavioral goals or who are brainstorming a Service Learning Project (see p. 116). You and the student can complete the Goal Setting Postcard together. You can revisit the postcard with the student weekly to offer support and/or until the goal has been realized.

## Title: Partner Mirroring

**Extended Script ✓ Activity**

**Provide students with the "Why" of the activity:** Today, we are learning **Partner Mirroring** to practice **community-building, managing our vulnerability, and peer-to-peer non-verbal communication**. This activity also helps us stay healthy by getting us up and out of our seats to take a movement break.

**Supplies:** Sentence strip to add the activity to the POP Chart
Music

**Time:** 7 minutes

**First:** Arrange the students into pairs. Instruct the students who will be going first (i.e. longer/shorter hair, birthday closest/furthest from today, etc.). Explain to the students that when the music starts, the designated partner will begin to move his body, while the other partner follows. The partners can use arms, legs, voices (sounds), but no speaking or directing.

**Then:** Ask students to stand facing a partner. When the music starts, the first student moves her body as the other student mirrors the movement. After about 10 seconds, loudly say "Switch" to cue the students that the leader switches. Continue for a few rounds.

**Next:** After a few rounds, cue the group: "Work collaboratively to make your group bigger without talking." (At this point, the pair will usually link up with one or two other pairs to form a small group.) Continue to loudly say "Switch" to cue the partners to rotate who is leading. (Remember, the groups must stay non-verbal. They cannot use words to direct others.) This continues for a few rounds, until each person has had a chance to lead.

**Last:** Continue to cue the groups to make their group bigger until the entire class is in one, large group. The teacher loudly says "Switch" a few more times, then slowly turns the music down. The teacher then takes over, moving the group at a slower pace, until the energy is calm, relaxed, and ready for the students to return to their seats.

★ **Teacher Tip:** If music is not being used, cue the group verbally: "Show me … [high/low, arms only/legs only/heads only, a yoga pose, a dance move, or a feeling or emotion from the POP Chart such as Happy, Angry, Hungry, or Sad]." For early childhood learners or students with exceptionalities, keep the students in pairs (instead of advancing to a larger group size) and cue different movements with different styles of music such as classical, folk, salsa, etc.

## Title: Compliment Partners

**Extended Script ✓ Activity**

**Provide students with the "Why" of the activity:** Today, we are practicing **Compliment Partners** to help us manage vulnerability and develop our **active listening and community-building skills**. This activity also helps us stay healthy by getting us up and out of our seats to take a movement break.

**Supplies:** Sentence strip to add the activity to the POP Chart
Clock or timer

**Time:** 5 minutes

**First:** Play music and ask your students to move around the room filling negative space (i.e. moving to open areas where no else is standing). When the music stops, cue the students to find the partner that is closest to her. Ask the students to stand facing their classmate, about arms-width apart.

**Then:** The teacher announces which student in the pair will go first (longer/shorter hair, birthday closest to today, bigger/smaller shoe size, etc.). That student will compliment her partner by witnessing a time that the other student was exhibiting a positive SEL social behavior such as being kind, compassionate, caring, a team player, a good listener, or thinking about solutions instead of problems.

**Next:** Give each partner 45 seconds to share a compliment before the music begins again and the students find new partners. Before the partners separate, cue the students to "hug, high five, or fist pound your partner to show her respect for what she shared with you today." Continue the activity for three more rounds.

**Last:** To close the activity, ask the students to return silently to their seats. Write "I am _____" on the board. Cue the students to turn one compliment that they received into an "I am" statement such as "I am kind," or "I am smart." To close the activity, the students will practice a mini-meditation. For 1 minute, they will breathe in and breathe out their "I am" statement, as if it were on a continuous loop in their minds. Once the students have their "I am" statements, ask them to sit up tall, shoulders rolled back, and eyes closed, and set the timer for 1 minute.

★ **Teacher Tip:** For the compliment sharing component of this activity to be successful, it is important you appropriately frame the activity by discussing the difference between a true, observational compliment and a joke or self-deprecating comment. A true compliment might be: "You are a kind person because you always include the third-grade students at recess, Anita. My little brother is in that recess period and I know that he is sometimes afraid of playing with the older kids," instead of: "You are really good at including younger kids at recess, Anita, even though no one really wants them to play with us. I wouldn't do that, but that's because I am not as nice as you are. I mean, I don't really think the younger kids are cool, so I wouldn't worry about including them." Or, "You are a very thoughtful and punctual person because you are always on time when we meet in the morning to walk to school," instead of, "I like that you are on time more now because you used to be lazy and show up late, and that was really annoying because I hated standing there waiting for you."

## Title: Shoulder Share*

**Extended Script ✓ Activity**

**Provide students with the "Why" of the activity:** Today, we are practicing **Shoulder Share** to continue to develop our **active listening skills and compassion for self and others**. This activity also helps us stay healthy by giving us an opportunity to get up and out of our seats.

**Supplies:** Sentence strip to add the activity to the POP Chart
Clock or timer

**Time:** 5 minutes

**First:** Write an SEL prompt on the board that you would like the students to discuss, such as ways in which to manage vulnerability, how to be compassionate with self and others, or ways in which to build community. Play music and ask your students to move around the room, filling negative space (i.e. moving to open areas where no else is standing). When the music stops, cue the students to find a partner that is closest to them. Each student is standing shoulder to shoulder with a classmate, facing the opposite direction (not making eye contact).

**Then:** The teacher announces which student in the pair will go first (longer/shorter hair, birthday closest to today, bigger/smaller shoe size, etc.). That student will be the first speaker to respond to the teacher's prompt.

**Next:** Give each partner 1 minute to share her thoughts. When the speaker is sharing, the listener does not speak. She does not offer an opinion or advice, she simply listens to the speaker. Once the minute concludes, the speaker and listener switch. Before the music begins again and the students find new partners, cue the students to "hug, high five, or fist pound your partner to show respect for him and what he shared with you today." Continue the activity for three more rounds.

**Last:** Ask the students to return silently to their seats. To close the activity, the students will practice a mini-meditation. For 1 minute, they will silently breathe in and breathe out a single sentence related to the prompt, such as "Teamwork is _____," or "Active Listening looks like _____," as if it were on a continuous loop in their minds. Ask the students to sit up tall, shoulders rolled back, and eyes closed, and set the timer for 1 minute.

★ **Teacher Tip:** As a great stress management activity prior to test taking, have the students share a worrisome thought or feeling regarding the upcoming test, such as, "I am afraid I am going to fail the writing section," or, "I hate math and I know I am going to do a terrible job on the math section!" Instruct each partner to respond by asking a follow-up question such as "What can I do to help you in this situation?" For early childhood learners, or students with exceptionalities, invite students to sit back to back or to hold a stuffed animal while sharing with their partner. This will minimize disruptions by keeping busy hands occupied and will help students focus on listening actively without interrupting.

* Adapted from Kripalu's Co-Listening Activity.

# 7

# SOCIAL Activities:
# Cool Down and Focus

The activities in this chapter are written for kindergarten to fifth-grade classrooms, with modifications suggested throughout for early childhood learners and students with exceptionalities. These activities are designed to be included in your classroom POP Chart in the "SOCIAL: Cool Down and Focus" quadrant.

As they are practiced in a group setting, these SOCIAL: Cool Down and Focus activities are designed to engage students interpersonally and center their energy through reflection and relaxation.

After each activity has been taught, it should be added to the POP Chart, so you can utilize it any time throughout the day when your class needs to focus and get In the Zone.

## Title: Positive Paperchain

**Extended Script ✓ Activity**

**Provide students with the "Why" of the activity:** We are creating a **Positive Paperchain** today to help us let go of negativity and **focus on the positive** aspects of our character. Positive Paperchain helps us be compassionate with ourselves and others.

**Supplies:** Sentence strip to add the activity to the POP Chart
Staplers
Multi-colored strips of construction paper
Pens and pencils

**Time:** 10 minutes

Read the directions below aloud while your students follow along. Remind students that the paperchain supplies are available so that they are able to add to the paperchain as part of their morning check-in routine or when they go to the POP Chart throughout the day.

**First:** Ask the students to take a deep breath, and think of a reason they are proud of themselves today, such as being active listeners, being responsible, or working well with others.

**Then:** Instruct the students to write a few sentences on their strip of construction paper that celebrates their strengths.

**Next:** Cue the students to review what they wrote, and breathe in feelings of positivity and pride.

**Last:** Passing around a few staplers, the students will join their paper with others' strips to create a colorful paper chain.

> ★ **Teacher Tip:** Grow the paperchain around the room all year. It is a great visual reminder of the positive energy that the classroom community has shared. As the teacher, feel free to add to the paperchain at any point throughout the week when you observe something positive in your classroom: "I received a wonderful report from our sub yesterday. Thank you, Room 410! I am going to add a positive thought to our paperchain!" Celebrating positivity and owning your strengths are great practices to model for your students.

## Title: Boom Board!

**Extended Script ✓ Activity**

**Provide students with the "Why" of the activity:** We are practicing **Boom Board!** today to **celebrate the positive qualities of our classroom community**. Often complimenting our classmates can be difficult, not only because it requires open peer-to-peer communication, but also because we have to manage our vulnerabilities. Boom Board! is a great way to showcase how unique and special our class is! Boom Board! supplies are available in the [location] so you can add to it as part of our morning check-in routine or whenever you visit the POP Chart throughout the day.

**Supplies:** Sentence strip to add the activity to the POP Chart
Small wall or bulletin board space with Boom Board! sign
Multi-colored sticky notes
Pens and pencils

**Time:** 3 minutes

Read the directions below aloud while your students follow along. Then, once the practice is established, include Boom Board! as part of your students' morning check-in routine.

**First:** Take a deep breath, and think of a reason you are proud of one of your classmates, such as for being a compassionate friend, helping someone in need, or being adaptable in a tough situation.

**Then:** On your sticky note, give that person a Boom! In other words, write a few sentences witnessing that person's strengths, kindness, or accomplishments. Your sentence might sound like: "Boom to Nelda for helping the foreign exchange student find her classroom this morning," or "Boom to Luca for solving the case of the missing water bottles during yesterday's field trip to the museum!"

**Next:** Review what you wrote, and breathe in feelings of community, collaboration, teamwork and pride.

**Last:** Sign and date your sticky note. Place it up on the Boom Board! to celebrate our classroom community.

★ **Teacher Tip:**

◆ Close your week by collecting the sticky notes off the Boom Board! and reading three to five notes aloud to the class. If possible, try to vary which students are acknowledged each week.

◆ File the Booms! from week to week in your students' files. Then, during state testing week, place one of those Booms! on each student's desk, to help them manage stress, self-doubt, and negative internal dialogue that may arise during testing time.

◆ Utilize the Boom Board! throughout the school day when you witness students helping one another, being compassionate, or collaborating: "I noticed Fez helping his group clean up their station. I am going to add Fez to the Boom Board! for awesome teamwork!" And, most importantly, encourage students to do the same: "Jackson, thank you for sharing with me that Willie included you at his lunch table today, when your tablemates were being rude to you. Jackson, would you like to add Willie to our Boom Board?"

◆ Employ Boom Board! throughout the school day when students are having a difficult time discerning between instructional and non-instructional questions. For instance, if a student interrupts your instruction to say "I love your earrings, Ms. Wong!", instead of addressing the comment and losing the pace of your instruction, you reply, "Thank you, LaTonya. But that sounds like a comment for our Boom Board!" While it is difficult to not return a compliment to a student, it is important that students learn they cannot interrupt your instruction with a series of non-instructional comments.

◆ For early childhood learners or students with exceptionalities, photocopy a template with a smiley face, a space for students to draw their Boom!, and a line to write their names. Have a sample posted near the Boom Board! for students to reference. This helps make the activity accessible for students with limited writing proficiency.

## Title: Pants on Fire!

**Extended Script ✓ Activity**

**Provide students with the "Why" of the activity:** We are practicing **Pants on Fire!** today to help us communicate urgent, troubling matters that are preventing us from being present, feeling emotionally or physically safe, or being Ready to Learn. Often, having difficult conversations or bringing up problems can be challenging, not only because it requires open peer-to-peer communication, but also because it requires that we manage our emotions. Pants on Fire! is **an excellent communication tool for appropriately sharing negative, troubling, or worrying thoughts**, feelings, and concerns.

**Supplies:** Sentence strip to add the activity to the POP Chart
Small wall or bulletin board space with Pants on Fire! sign
Multi-colored sticky notes
Pens and pencils

**Time:** 3 minutes

Read the directions below aloud while your students follow along. Remind students that supplies for Pants on Fire! are available so that they are able to add to Pants on Fire! as part of their morning check-in routine or when they go to the POP Chart throughout the day.

**First:** Take a deep breath, and think of a reason you are feeling triggered or activated, such as being upset that something is seemingly unfair, being concerned that something appears unsafe, needing help in a tough situation, or needing to express a negative feeling or emotion you are experiencing.

**Then:** On your sticky note, write a few sentences explaining your concern. Your sentence might sound like, "I am upset that I missed breakfast this morning. I am hungry and I cannot concentrate," or "I am worried about our math test this afternoon because I left my homework at my dad's and couldn't study." Notice, there are only "I" statements on the Pants on Fire! board. You may not use other students' names in your Pants on Fire! This is not a place to tattle. You only write about what YOU are experiencing that is keeping YOU from being focused and Ready to Learn.

**Next:** Review what you wrote, and take a deep breath in. Notice how you feel seeing the words on the paper. Notice if there is anything else you need to write to be able to let go, focus, and be Ready to Learn.

**Last:** Sign and date your sticky note and post it to the board before you take your seat. The teacher will read the Pants on Fire! board throughout the week. Some items the teacher may want to talk to you about, such as if it is too cold in the room and you can't concentrate. But realize, Pants on Fire! is a communication tool. Your teacher may not be able to solve every problem that is on the board. It simply gives you an outlet to communicate anything that is keeping you from being Ready to Learn.

★ **Teacher Tip:**

◆ Walk past Pants on Fire! a few times each day to get a sense of what your students are experiencing that they may/may not be able to articulate. Follow up with students on urgent or timely items.

◆ Remind students that Pants on Fire! is a communication tool. Even though the teacher cares very much, she may not be able to solve every problem that appears on the board.

◆ File Pants on Fires! from week to week in your students' files. Then, during parent teacher conferences, you have a reminder of reoccurring themes that may help inform your conversations with parents.

◆ Utilize Pants on Fire! throughout the school day when students are having a difficult time discerning between instructional and non-instructional questions. For instance, if a student interrupts your instruction to say, "I don't have a new bus schedule. I need to call my mom and tell her when to pick me up!", instead of addressing the question and losing the pace of your instruction, you reply, "Arnold, that sounds like a Pants on Fire! to me. When we finish this next problem, you can grab a sticky note and add that to Pants on Fire!" It is important that students learn they cannot interrupt your instruction with non-instructional questions or comments.

◆ For early childhood learners or students with exceptionalities, photocopy a template with a frowning face, a space for students to draw their concern, and a line to write their names. Have a sample posted near the Pants on Fire! board for students to reference. This helps make the activity accessible for students with limited writing proficiency.

## Title: Kind Kid Postcard

**Extended Script ✓ Activity**

**Provide students with the "Why" of the activity:** We are creating **Kind Kid Postcards** today to reinforce community-building and self-esteem. This activity empowers us to find our voices and **witness our kind, compassionate selves** as well as be kind and compassionate towards others.

**Supplies:** Sentence strip to add the activity to the POP Chart
4 × 6 index cards, lined on one side
Postage stamps (optional)
Pens and pencils

**Time:** 7 minutes

To begin, distribute 4 × 6 index cards to your students. Then, read the directions below aloud while your students follow along.

**First:** Take a deep breath, and think of a reason you are proud of yourself, such as for being an attentive listener, a compassionate friend, or a good group leader.

**Then:** On the front of the index card (the side with lines), write a few sentences, or draw a picture, to illustrate why you are proud of yourself.

**Next:** Complete the back of the postcard (the side without lines), writing the reason you are proud of yourself today. Don't forget to sign and date your postcard!

**Last:** Address your postcard to someone with whom you would like to share your positive thoughts, such as a former teacher, a parent, your dean, or a community member.

★ **Teacher Tip:** Once the postcards are complete, you can save postage by distributing the school-bound postcards to your colleagues' mailboxes after school. For early childhood learners or students with exceptionalities, photocopy a template with a space for students to draw and a line to write their names. Draw a sample on the board for your students to reference. This helps make the activity accessible for students with limited writing proficiency.

## Title: Talking Stick

### Extended Script ✓ Activity

**Provide students with the "Why" of the activity:** We are practicing Talking Stick to learn how to appropriately express emotions, enhance **peer-to-peer communication**, and increase Social Awareness.

**Supplies:** Sentence strip to add the activity to the POP Chart

Any soft object that can be passed from student to student (a large, bulky stuffed animal or something that is not easy to throw).

**Time:** 7 minutes

The basic premise of this activity is that the person who is holding the stick gets to speak. Although this is a simple principle, to guarantee that a Talking Stick session is an emotionally safe experience for students, it is good to create Agreements for use. These Agreements can extend to general sharing, class meetings, or any other large group discussions.

It is recommended that you laminate your Talking Stick Agreements and place them next to the POP Chart in your classroom. Before the Talking Stick session begins, the teacher should write the start and end time on the board. A typical time frame is 3–5 minutes, but the amount of time may vary depending on topic, time of day, etc. For example, Start: 9:15 am, End: 9:18 am.

While each classroom is different, below are a few recommendations for creating your Talking Stick Agreements (for guidelines on creating general classroom Agreements, see p. 42):

- The person holding the Talking Stick is the only one to speak. Each speaker may share for no longer than 30 seconds. [The teacher should establish a non-verbal sign, such as three snaps in the air, to signify when the speaker's time has concluded.]
- The Talking Stick is passed silently from speaker to speaker, in the order in which students raised their hands to share. [The Talking Stick is not to be thrown or simply given to the person closest to the speaker.] The silence between speakers is the perfect time for the class to reflect on what was being shared. It is recommended that each speaker take an easy breath, with eyes closed, to collect her thoughts before speaking.

◆ Describe listening expectations for a Talking Stick session. What does active listening look like and sound like in this setting?

◆ The speaker must wait until two more classmates have spoken before they request to speak again. The speaker understands that there may not be enough time for them to have another turn.

◆ The speaker must use "I" language and talk only about their experiences and opinions. It is important that everyone feels comfortable sharing. A Talking Stick Session is judgment-free. [Also include no piggybacking, or restating someone else's point. This guideline often leads to more original and diverse thinking on an issue.]

◆ Each Talking Stick Session should conclude with a one-word check-in. If time is tight, the teacher can simply choose three to five people, ideally those that did not get a chance to share during the session, to share one word about their feelings and thoughts on the topic. [Please instruct the students that their one word is a reflection of the topic or about the overall experience of being in community, not about the people that shared.]

★ **Teacher Tip:** Use the Talking Stick to have friends work out a conflict (timed) or in groups where there is difficulty building consensus (start with the student with the longest hair and move around the group). Make the Talking Stick available to students during their morning check-in routine. They may walk in with positive or negative information to process. Giving them a positive outlet to share that information not only reinforces effective communication practices in a social setting, it also gives students the tools to be focused, present, and Ready to Learn. Before starting the Talking Stick session, manage students' expectations by giving them a start/end time and an estimation of how many students will have a chance to share.

## Title: Cotton Ball Breathing

**Extended Script ✓ Activity**

**Provide students with the "Why" of the activity:** We are practicing **Cotton Ball Breathing** to **explore the connections between breath, body**, and Social Awareness. Cotton Ball Breathing builds awareness of ourselves and our environment through a focus on working together.

**Supplies:** Sentence strip to add the activity to the POP Chart
Bag of cotton balls

**Time:** 7 minutes

**First:** Pass out one cotton ball per student, and assign each student a partner. Depending on their height, have the partners sit or stand facing one another. Instruct the partners to extend opposite hands, palms up, so their fingertips touch. Remind students to always keep their palms flat.

**Then:** The teacher announces which student in the pair will go first (longer/shorter hair, birthday closest to today, bigger/smaller shoe size, etc.). That student will place the cotton ball in her hand while the other partner holds his hand out empty. The partners then take turns blowing the cotton ball from the palm of their hands to their partner's. Repeat three times.

**Next:** Draw the attention to the students' breath. "If we use a powerful exhalation, the cotton ball travels farther. If we use a soft exhalation, the cotton ball travels a shorter distance. Throughout the course of the activity, observe the length of your inhalations compared to your exhalations. Notice how they change and how they stay the same. Also, notice how you and your partner must use teamwork and body awareness to successfully move the cotton ball from one hand to the other." Once each partner has had a turn, cue the partners to separate and move back to their seats. When seated, each student needs enough personal space so that he can sit with his arms extended into a "T" position.

**Last:** Each student places the cotton ball in the palm of one hand and places the other hand on his desk. Keeping their feet flat on the floor, their shoulders rolled back, and palms flat, the students attempt to blow the cotton ball from the palms of their hands to their fingertips, without it rolling off their palms and falling on to the desk. As they practice, cue the students to continuously slow their breath down so the cotton ball barely moves in their hands. Repeat five times.

★ **Teacher Tip:** This is an excellent activity to use prior to a test, as it redirects student attention. If time permits, cue your students to form groups of four or five. Each student places their right hand in the center with fingertips touching, making a flower-like shape. Their job, as a group, is to blow the cotton ball from hand to hand, keeping it from touching the floor.

## Title: Color Breath

**Extended Script ✓ Activity**

**Provide students with the "Why" of the activity:** We are practicing **Color Breath** to explore the **connections between breath, body**, and Social Awareness. Color Breath builds awareness of ourselves and our environment through a focus on the breath.

**Supplies:** Sentence strip to add the activity to the POP Chart

**Time:** 3 minutes

**First:** Sit in an easy, cross-legged position, or sit at your desk with both feet flat on the floor.

**Then:** I will choose a student who has modeled positive behavior today to pick his favorite color. (Select a student, and have him share his favorite color.)

**Next:** Let's all take a deep breath and close our eyes.

**Last:** Exhaling together, let's chant the color chosen. (For example: "Grrreeeeeeeeeeennn.")

## Title: Bee's Breath

**Extended Script ✓ Activity**

**Provide students with the "Why" of the activity:** We are practicing **Bee's Breath** to explore the **connections between breath, body**, and Social Awareness. Bee's Breath builds awareness of ourselves and our environment through a focus on the breath.

**Supplies:** Sentence strip to add the activity to the POP Chart

**Time:** 3 minutes

**First:** Sit at your desk with your shoulders rolled back and your feet flat on the floor.

**Then:** Close your eyes, and put your hands over your ears.

**Next:** Take a deep breath. Exhaling to the count of four, make a buzzing sound together like a bunch of bees.

**Last:** Keep your eyes closed and let's repeat Bee's Breath four times together.

## Title: Community-Based Service Learning Project

**Extended Script ✓ Activity**

**Provide students with the "Why" of the activity:** We are planning and participating in a **Service Learning Project** to connect with our community by sharing thoughts and resources. In our SEL program this year we have worked hard to cultivate our sense of **Self-Efficacy and Social Harmony by developing our leadership, collaboration, teamwork, and peer-to-peer communication skills**. This year, we have worked on Being the Solution for ourselves and our school. Now, to demonstrate our Social-Emotional Learning skills, we will create a Service Learning Project to Be the Solution for our community.

**Supplies:** To be determined based upon project chosen

**Estimated Project Time:** 3–4 weeks

**Service Learning Project:** Having students work collaboratively to create a Service Learning Project is the perfect way to reinforce a sense of community. Service Learning Projects are most successful when they bring different groups together, such as one classroom partnering with an older/younger grade to create a school "Green Space" or to put on a play at the local senior center.

This project can become a growth narrative for the class and a reflection tool that validates their ability to foster effective interpersonal communication, to seize opportunities for self-reflection, and to accept the needs and limits of self and others.

Prior to the start of the project, it is important to message the concept of responsible giving and/or "giving back" to the community. Instead of framing the service learning project as a one-sided proposition of "us" helping "them," discuss the ways in which "giving back" to the community creates an opportunity for the class to contemplate their role within the community, to share their voice with community members, to collaborate in the creation of something meaningful and relevant and to engage in a relationship of reciprocal learning. It is also crucial that the students set goals around the project, measure its impact and examine prospects for sustainability, thus moving away from monetary gifts and moving toward "Being the Solution" and "giving back" via human connection.

★ **Teacher Tip:** Some states, such as Illinois, have Service Learning Standards that connect nicely to their Social-Emotional Learning standards (in this case, most notably, "Goal 3 – Demonstrate decision-making skills and responsible behaviors in personal, school, and community contexts"). Connecting these standards can be a great way to create metrics to measure the overall impact of the project. This project is also an excellent opportunity to build bridges between regular education students and students with exceptionalities!

# 8

# Crafting SEL Stories

Our Mindful Practices program model begins with a lesson each Monday, which includes an SEL Story to make relevant connections between Social-Emotional Learning and students' lives.

The SEL Story is an instrumental element of each Monday's Social-Emotional Learning lesson. It is not just the reading of the story or the theme of the story itself, it is the peer-to-peer communication tools employed during the activity that are the richest and most impactful aspect.

There are two options for how the teacher could implement the SEL Story.

## Option 1: Be the Solution Teams
The students work in teams to decide a solution to a culturally relevant SEL problem or issue taken from the Thumbs-Up/Thumbs-Down Box.

## Option 2: Class Dialogue
The teacher uses one of the templates from pages 124 or 125 to create a culturally relevant SEL Story based upon problems or issues taken from the Thumbs-Up/Thumbs-Down Box. Or, the teacher reads one of the scripted SEL Stories provided and facilitates a reflective dialogue with the students.

Before choosing which option will work best, reflect on happenings in the school community that may or may not need to be addressed. Look at the interpersonal needs of your students and what would best serve them today. Look at the time available for your lesson: the pacing of the activity is important and should not be rushed, as it will lose its reflective potency.

As the teacher delivering the lesson, reflect on your own SEL competency around the topic. What lessons have you learned that you can share with your students? What are your current challenges and areas of growth around the topic?

Implementation steps for both SEL Options are outlined below. Some of the SEL terminology embedded in the Sample Stories (p. 126) is shown in **bold** to make it easy to emphasize while teaching and to help the teacher create an SEL word wall. Transparency is key for SEL to take root in students' lives. The terminology should be used as part of a common classroom language during SEL instruction and across disciplines and should be reinforced throughout the day.

## Delivery of SEL Stories

Step 1: Look at the POP Chart. Where did the majority of students place their magnets? Which emotion or feeling is most represented in your class today and what do your students need to be Ready to Learn?

Step 2: Choose SEL Story format (either Option 1: Be the Solution Teams (p. 122) or option 2: SEL Class Dialogue (p. 124).

Step 3: Close SEL Story experience with an activity from the POP Chart to help your class get focused and Ready to Learn.

> ★ **Teacher Tip:** Close with a SELF or SOCIAL activity from the POP Chart, like Memory Minute (p. 84). Remember, there are two choices for how you would like to implement the SEL Story, either in Be the Solution Teams or as a Class Dialogue, depending on your students' needs and the time you have available that day.

Remember, there are two options for how you would like to implement the SEL Story, either in Be the Solution Teams or as a Class Dialogue, depending on your students' needs and the time you have available that day.

## Message the "Why" to Your Students

Below is a scripted lesson for introducing the SEL Stories to your students. As with the other scripted lessons in this book, it is **not** recommended that you read the script aloud word for word, as that would not help develop your competency as a practitioner. Instead, the script is meant to provide a solid idea of how the content is framed, paced, and managed. Read the script a few times, take notes, and then make it your own.

[Teacher writes Social-Emotional Learning on the board.] As part of our Social-Emotional Learning program in Room [x] we will share real-life stories about Social-Emotional Learning every Monday. We will explore a new story or theme every week and discuss how it relates to Social-Emotional Learning and our own experiences as students at [x] Elementary School. Some Mondays, when big things are happening at school or in our community, we will get into Be the Solutions teams and discuss our SEL Story. Other Mondays, we will have conversation about the SEL Story and try to understand the story from different points of view. It is very important that the concepts and themes we discuss are relevant to you. Remember, you can always add a theme, idea, or concern to our Thumbs-Up/ Thumbs-Down box if you would like me to include it as an SEL topic next week. Also, remember that we have the POP Chart to help us **PAUSE** and notice what we are feeling in the body and the mind. [Teacher motions to POP Chart.] Next, we identify and **OWN** what we are feeling. Then, we choose an activity from the POP Chart so we can **PRACTICE** regulating our behavior and making positive choices that are good for ourselves and our classroom community. We are in control of our choices. We can Be the Solution!

To review, every Monday our SEL practice will consist of:

1. A Morning Pop Chart Check-In
2. A Social-Emotional Learning Story

Tuesday – Friday our SEL practice will consist of:

1. A Morning Pop Chart Check-In
2. A SELF or SOCIAL Activity to add to our POP Chart

Additionally, the POP Chart activities are there at any time, if we need to Get In the Zone and energize or relax either as individuals or as a class.

Does anyone have any questions about our SEL stories or our SEL time each week?

# SEL Story: Option 1

## Title: Be the Solution Teams

**Teacher Script ✓ Activity**

**Provide students with the "Why" of the activity:** Today, we will be using our creative thinking skills to come up with solutions for a Social-Emotional Learning scenario that was put in the Thumbs-Up/Thumbs-Down box. By working as a team to come up with a solution, we are using our **problem solving and collaboration skills**. When we are discussing solutions, let's remember the tools we have learned using the POP Chart. Before we get started, we will be practicing a quick centering activity, so we have productively used our extra energy and can focus and work as a team.

> ★ **Teacher Tip:** The script for creating the Agreements mentioned below is on page 42, and would be a great way to create a safe space for this activity.

**First:** Select a student who is exhibiting Be the Solution behavior to lead the class through Seated Arm Stretch (p. 61) for 10 breaths with their eyes closed.

Practicing a quick centering activity is a great way to help the class release excess energy that can often make working in a group challenging for your more frenetic students.

**Then:** Write an SEL Scenario from the Thumbs-Up/Thumbs-Down Box on the board with two or three possible solutions. Place students in groups of four or five, and designate a Recorder and a First Speaker (choosing e.g. a student with the shortest/longest hair, shortest first/last name or birthday closest/furthest from today). When you say "Begin," the First Speaker will have 1 minute to share his opinion on which scenario is the best solution to the problem, while the Recorder takes notes.

**Next:** At the end of the minute, say "Switch" and, moving counter-clockwise, the next student in the group will share his thoughts. This continues for five rounds, until each student has had a chance to speak. While the group is sharing, the Recorder is taking notes.

**Last:** Once the rounds have concluded, give the groups 3 minutes to synthesize their information to present to the class. The Recorder will read her notes. Starting again with the First Speaker, the group will take turns adding any additional thoughts or solutions. When time is up, each group will have 1 minute to share their thoughts with the class. The Recorder may speak, or choose someone in the group to speak in her place.

★ **Teacher Tips:** Decide how you would like to conclude the discussion. Did the class build consensus around a solution that you would like to add to your classroom Agreements? Would you like to revisit the process of adding a thought, concern, or idea to the Thumbs-Up/Thumbs-Down Box as a way to inform the procedures and protocols of the classroom (and school) community? How can you engineer this activity to be both productive and reflective for you and the students? If there is space, perhaps keep an on-going list of SEL competencies your class is practicing. Instead of the static "theme of the week," make this a living, breathing list that you are adding to, speaking to, and referencing throughout the week.

## Making it Relevant

In order for this exercise to have impact, students must feel the activity was relevant to their lives and has an effect on their immediate circumstances. The role of the teacher is key here to build consensus and keep transitions tight. Besides the major benefits of tailor making relevant SEL content for your classroom, the speaking and listening inherent in this activity are great for building interpersonal relationships among students.

This is an excellent activity for helping students take ownership of their behavior and find solutions in real time. For instance, if your students misbehave at an assembly, when you return to your classroom, put the students in their Be the Solution Teams and have them build consensus around a consequence and/or solution. This not only helps students develop a sense of personal responsibility, but it also helps them see the impact of their actions, both positive and negative, on the classroom community.

## SEL Class Dialogue: Option 2

Use the Thumbs-Up/Thumbs-Down Box and the templates below to write SEL Stories for your students. The more culturally relevant the stories are to the students' lives, the larger the impact. Sample reflection questions are also provided to conclude each lesson. If you are having a difficult time getting started, I have also included 6 sample stories later in the chapter.

### Template 1

_____ (culturally relevant character name) is in the _____ grade at _____ school. _____ (name) found herself in a difficult situation today. She _____ (name difficult situation). Because she was upset, _____ (name) _____ (negative action), which is not a positive step toward a solution. How can _____ (name) use our one of the techniques in the POP Chart to make a more positive choice? What solution would be a more positive choice for _____ (name) and her class?

### Template 2

Today, _____ (culturally relevant character name) used poor decision-making skills and got into trouble for _____. He knows that it is his personal responsibility to resolve the situation. Unfortunately, he _____(negative action), which only made the problem worse. Now _____ (name) does not know how to improve the situation. What is a positive way for _____ (name) to take responsibility for his actions and find a solution? What Social-Emotional Learning tools or techniques from our POP Chart could help him in this situation?

**Template 3**

Room _____ misbehaved today in _____. Their teacher is disappointed, because she knows that if they used better peer-to-peer communication and active listening skills, Room _____ could have made more positive choices about their behavior. To resolve the situation, Room _____ needs to reflect on their decision-making skills and use teamwork to find a positive next step. What are two positive steps that Room _____ could take to resolve the situation? How can they use Social-Emotional Learning or mindfulness strategies to find the most positive path?

## Student Reflection Questions

When teaching your story each week, make sure to conclude the lesson with the reflection questions below:

May I have a volunteer to tell me what happens in the story? [Teacher asks one student to explain the story.]

There are a few different ways that _____ (student name/s) could use our SEL or mindfulness techniques in the story. May I have two volunteers to share ideas of how _____ (student name/s) could make more positive choices and better cope with their difficult situation? [Teacher asks two students to connect the SEL Story to the activities in the POP Chart. Once the students conclude, the teacher rephrases their explanations in 1–2 sentences.]

> ★ **Teacher Tip:** While teaching your SEL Story, remember to write the SEL terms on the board and/or add them to your SEL word wall to embed in your instruction throughout the week! SEL is most impactful when it connects directly to students' lives. Make it relevant. Make it matter!

## Sample SEL Stories

SEL words are shown in **bold**, for the teachers to reinforce throughout the day during instruction, add to their SEL word walls, or include in correspondence home to parents and caregivers.

1. Violet was **upset** with three kids in her class who were always misbehaving at recess and had a difficult time controlling their behavior. If Violet's class continued to **behave poorly** at recess their class trip was going to be taken away. Violet knew they were going to ruin it for everyone else! When these three students **behaved poorly**, Violet tried yelling "Shut up" or giving them the silent treatment, but nothing seemed to work. Then one day, Violet tried to **talk respectfully** to each of the students about not ruining the field trip for everyone else. The talk was very challenging, but one by one the three students began to **see how their behavior was negatively impacting** their class' chance to go on the fieldtrip.

*May I have a volunteer to tell me what happens in the story? [Teacher asks one student to explain the story.]*

*Now, may I have two volunteers explain which techniques Violet could have used to help her **manage her anger** with her classmates and appropriately **express her emotions** without yelling "Shut up!"? [Teacher asks two students to connect the SEL Story to the activities in the POP Chart. Once the students conclude, the teacher closes the activity by rephrasing their explanations in 1–2 sentences.]*

2. Patrick came home from school upset because a friend of his wasn't nice to him at lunch. He knew from the **heavy feeling in his stomach and the tightness in his chest** that he was **holding a lot of hurt feelings in his body**. He knew he could make himself feel better if he thought about something he did well that day, practiced a **breathing activity**, or engaged in a **physical activity**, such as dancing or playing soccer with his neighbors.

*May I have a volunteer to tell me what happens in the story? [Teacher asks one student to explain the story.]*

*Now, may I have two volunteers explain what techniques Patrick can practice to help him develop **emotional and body awareness**? [Teacher asks two students* *to connect the SEL Story to the activities in the POP Chart. Once the students conclude, the teacher closes the activity by rephrasing their explanations in 1–2 sentences.]*

3. Shakita left her spelling words at her mom's apartment and she didn't get a chance to study. She missed four words on her spelling test the next day. She was very **angry with herself.** In fact, she was so angry that she **couldn't focus** on her Math quiz and even messed up in PE class later that afternoon. Shakita knows that she needs to **productively manage her emotions** and be **compassionate with herself,** but she doesn't quite know how.

*May I have a volunteer to tell me what happens in the story? [Teacher asks one student to explain the story.]*

*Now, may I have two volunteers explain which techniques Shakita can practice to help her **manage her anger and better cope with frustrating situations?** [Teacher asks two students to connect the SEL Story to the activities in the POP Chart. Once the students conclude, the teacher closes the activity by rephrasing their explanations in 1–2 sentences.]*

4. Precious has always hated Art and does not get along with her teacher, Ms. Jackson. Whenever she runs into a problem with one of her drawings or paintings, she **gives up** because she thinks it is too hard and that Ms. Jackson does not care if she succeeds. Precious was chosen by the principal to be part of her school's team at the city-wide Art fair. When she worked with the team and things got hard, she **wanted to give up,** but her teammates **depended on her** to participate. **Teamwork** is very important to Precious and so, even though she doesn't love Art, she **tried her best.** Precious' team won second place at the city-wide fair. She was proud of herself and her team.

*May I have a volunteer to tell me what happens in the story? [Teacher asks one student to explain the story.]*

*Now, may I have two volunteers explain which techniques Precious can practice to help her **manage feelings of frustration and focus on being part of the team?** [Teacher asks two students to connect the SEL Story to the activities in the POP Chart. Once the students conclude, the teacher closes the activity by rephrasing their explanations in 1–2 sentences.]*

5. LeAndra and Ellen are sitting in a circle with their classmates. LeAndra is sitting very close to Ellen and is playing with her hair. Ellen is **uncomfortable** and feels her **safe space is being violated**. It is important that LeAndra **respect her peers' personal space**. Instead of shoving LeAndra away or yelling "Eww – get off me!," Ellen politely asked LeAndra, "Can you please scoot over? I am feeling squished and would like more room." LeAndra apologized and, although it was bit awkward between them for a moment, she moved a few inches away without starting a fight.

*May I have a volunteer to tell me what happens in the story? [Teacher asks one student to explain the story.]*

*Now, may I have one volunteer explain what techniques LeAndra can practice to help her **develop personal responsibility and understanding of her behavioral choices**? May I have another volunteer explain how Ellen **found her voice** and **used her words to problem solve** the situation with LeAndra? [Teacher asks two students to connect the SEL Story to the activities in the POP Chart. Once the students conclude, the teacher closes the activity by rephrasing their explanations in 1–2 sentences.]*

6. Sometimes in school, Martin gets **angry** when he has his hand up and the teacher calls on another student. Martin is **aware** he is getting **frustrated**, because he can feel his ears getting red and his checks burning. But instead of blurting out the answer, rolling his eyes, or smacking his lips, he **takes a breath** and waits to raise his hand until the next question. Sometimes the teacher will call on him, and sometimes, because the class is so big, he doesn't get a turn.

*May I have a volunteer to tell me what happens in the story? [Teacher asks one student to explain the story.]*

*Now, may I have two volunteers explain which techniques Martin can practice to help him **manage his emotions and self-regulate**? [Teacher asks two students to connect the SEL Story to the activities in the POP Chart. Once the students conclude, the teacher closes the activity by rephrasing their explanations in 1–2 sentences.]*

# 9

# Cultivating Teacher Competency Through Professional Development

## Teacher Competency and Substantive Professional Development: The Missing Pieces to Impactful SEL Implementation

Imperfect SEL implementation has become the unfortunate industry standard in education. With the myriad of high-stakes testing issues currently thrown at teachers, why should they make time to learn SEL? SEL seems simple enough; why can't schools just adopt quick and easy programs where teachers read scripted material to their class and no one questions their efficacy or effectiveness?

Sure, schools can do that. And, by doing so, they can expect the same result that varying character education and SEL programs have gotten over the past few decades. After the initial sparkly charge, the implementation fades, leaving just the few go-getters scattered across the building. Why? Mainly, because it was "just another fad, just like a, b, or c that they all saw x number of years ago." To prevent this unfortunate and predictable phenomenon, SEL needs to be embedded into the school culture, with practices that span grade bands and content.

Before we begin to assemble that first SEL bulletin board, we must take a look at the SEL competency of the delivery vehicle, the teacher. As we know, if the delivery vehicle is faulty, the material is lost in translation. Often when I am touring a new school, a principal will say this teacher has "got it" or that teacher "doesn't." In teacher-speak, we all know what this statement means, and we have been complicit is letting it go at just that. The problem is that without codifying the practices that create a positive, safe, and emotionally respectful classroom, we leave ourselves unable to teach those who haven't quite "gotten it" yet. Our professional responsibility is to move away from sweeping and lofty expectations like "teaching respect" toward building teachers' SEL competency so they can develop common, explicit SEL language and practices for their classrooms. SEL instruction must dig deeper than simply looking at the number of students reached or the number of minutes taught. Instead, we must look at the competency of those who are the delivery vehicle for the SEL program itself. What is the climate and culture of the classroom in which the SEL program is housed? Is that classroom an emotionally and physically safe environment for SEL to take place, and can all learners, even our most vulnerable, thrive?

Teacher competency is a vital part of the successful implementation of a school-wide SEL program. If classroom teachers are expected to implement Social-Emotional Learning programs and state SEL standards with efficacy, proficiency cannot be assumed. Given that most teacher education programs lack sufficient pre-service training in SEL, teachers must receive high-quality SEL professional development, consistent support, and a safe space to reflect and to take risks.

Teachers know whether or not they are able to effectively teach trigonometry. They are either certified to teach math or they are not. In addition to looking at the competency of the educator, students' math assessments can be evaluated to determine that they either have or have not mastered the concept.

The process is not as simple for teaching and assessing SEL. Many of our nation's teachers were certified before SEL was included in the state standards and so it was not included in their teacher education programs. When addressing educators' SEL competency at a new school site, I often hear the question, "Are you saying that some teachers don't know how to effectively resolve a conflict? Or that they don't have Social Awareness?" And, as we have all seen by visiting a gossipy faculty lounge at lunchtime, sometimes that answer is obvious.

Teachers cannot effectively teach SEL without modeling the strategies. And they cannot effectively model what they are not competent in. Yet, at least half of the SEL instruction I see when I visit schools across the country is teachers pulling a card from a box or a lesson from a binder and "teaching their SEL minutes for the day." The teacher's self-reflective piece is completely absent and the impact of the program is diminished.

Understandably, the administrator, social worker, or teacher that purchased these kits wants to assume practitioner competency because the alternative is an awkward conversation at best and, at worst, the practitioner dismissing SEL as "one more thing they don't have time for," or "the flavor of the month," and refusing to address the content at all. Desperate to include SEL, schools often settle for the half-taught lesson in lieu of the content being abandoned all together.

The best practice here is to address the question of teacher competency prior to a district's program adoption and to either find a champion internally or to select a program provider who insists upon professional development as the cornerstone of an impactful and sustainable SEL program. Implementing an intentional and reflective professional development program is key. A "one-shot" train-the-trainer PD session is not enough, as there is only time to cover particular SEL strategies, not to evaluate the practitioner's overall mastery of the concepts. One can learn "Chopsticks" on the piano, but that does not mean one can model proper technique or knows how to effectively teach "Chopsticks" to someone else.

Intentional professional development gives teachers the space to view themselves through the SEL lens. Are they Self-Aware? Are they able to Self-Regulate? What triggers them while teaching and keeps them from being present and compassionate educators?

Unfortunately, Self-Awareness is often not part of the culture of expectations for teachers. There is a perfect storm that subverts teacher SEL competency: a high-stakes testing culture that doesn't make space for vulnerability paired with an emotion-adverse system that glorifies "busy." Busy instead of Reflective has become the mantra of schools. Our teachers often feel they are "running on fumes" and do not have time for "one more thing," even if implementing that one more thing – Social-Emotional Learning – would help them and their students be more engaged and thus achieve more (the very thing that is stressing teachers out in the first place). If teachers have not experienced the value of self-care or self-soothing, they won't find time for it in their classrooms. They won't see the connection between SEL and being Ready to Learn because they have not experienced it for themselves.

Teachers cannot model or teach Self-Awareness or Self-Regulation in a school culture that doesn't honor these concepts as values. As John Hattie astutely observes in his book, *Visible Learning: A Synthesis of Over 800 Meta-Analyses Relating to Achievement* (2009):

> School leaders and teachers need to create school, staffroom, and classroom environments where error is welcomed as a learning opportunity, where discarding incorrect knowledge and understandings is welcomed, and where participants can feel safe to learn, re-learn, and explore knowledge and understanding.

To build an impactful SEL program, the "incorrect knowledge" that teachers, just by virtue of being teachers, are SEL competent must be discarded. How could they be competent at something they have never been taught? Instead, provide teachers with a safe space to reflect on their own SEL competency, so they can develop mastery of the content they are expected to deliver.

## Building an Impactful Professional Development Experience

### Step 1: Recruit Your Principal

One of the jobs of an administrator is to create an emotionally and physically safe space for his team to have room to be creative, reflective, and to take risks. Teachers must be given permission to move away from the narrative of "too busy" or "too disenchanted" to care. We should frame this shift the same way we give the challenging student permission to reinvent his self-perpetuating label of "Class Clown," so that he can abandon the shackles of the narrative and grow into a more positive experience.

It is vital that the administration introduces the professional development (PD) program and message expectations around SEL at the school. With all the other things on teachers' plates at the start of the school year, why should they be expected to devote time to a 3-hour SEL professional development session? Why has the district allocated valuable resources for this work? What is our baseline? What are the expectations? What is the timeline? How is this connected to student achievement? And, of course, how will SEL be reflected in teacher evaluations?

If the principal is not ready to answer these questions, then the implementation will lack commitment. Implementing SEL with integrity takes strong leadership, consistently reinforced boundaries, difficult conversations, and clear vision.

This is a great opportunity to work alongside your principal to create the school's SEL plan. Before moving forward with implementation, take time to sit with your principal to discuss the questions below, so that you can deliver a clear and consistent message to the school stakeholders at the first professional development session.

*Question 1: The game plan*
What is your vision for our school's SEL program?

*Question 2: The timeline*
What is our timeline and what steps do we need to take to get there?

*Question 3: The measurement*
How do we track our progress to make sure we stay on course?

*Question 4: The team*
Who are the school SEL stakeholders that can lead the charge and help us create something sustainable?

*Question 5: The wish list*
What resources and support do we need to accomplish our vision?

*Question 6: Common language*
How do we frame SEL to our school community – teachers, bus drivers, parents, administrators, lunch monitors, recess facilitators, deans, social workers, etc. – so it reinforces the SEL vision for our school?

*Question 7: Call to Action*
In the Zone? Be the Solution? Ready to Learn? How can all school stake-holders consistently message expectations to our students?

*Question 8: Service Learning Project*
Brainstorm an end-of-year Service Learning Project that brings us into con-nection with our school community and reinforces SEL concepts, like team-work and compassion.

If the principal cannot be the leadership presence at each SEL professional development session, it is important that he chooses a strong facilitator to lead the charge and help participants Be In the Zone in his absence.

## Step 2: Choose a Strong Professional Development Facilitator

The role of the facilitator is of utmost importance for a successful profes-sional development session, for it is her job to create an emotionally and physically safe space for learning to take place. Often, when I am leading a PD session, I will have an observer say to me, "Well, um, do we really need the Agreements [see p. 137]? I mean, we are adults, after all, and some people might be offended." My answer is, predictably, YES.

Typically, it is those participants that are offended by the Agreements that need them the most. They are the participants who invade boundaries and make others feel uncomfortable or unsafe by grading papers when the facilitator is speaking, making rude comments under their breath, showing up late, chomping on a snack, or checking their phones – anything that keeps them from being present. All these actions send the message that they don't "need" the content and don't think it is worth their time to be there. The role of the facilitator takes courage. It takes guts. It takes grit and the willingness to have difficult conversations. No more "Well, that's just Coach Butler *being* Coach Butler." These participants are exhibiting behavior they would never tolerate from their students. It is the job of the facilitator to create boundaries and set limits, so that the professional development is safe for all.

Facilitators must be comfortable modeling the strategies during the PD session that they want their teachers to model in their classrooms, if they expect sustainable, school-wide implementation. Be the Solution, or your Call to Action, must apply to all stakeholders – no exceptions. A successful PD experience, facilitated in a safe environment by a strong, consistent voice, will pull disenfranchised teachers back into connection with one another and with their profession.

### Step 3: Create an Implementation Timeline for Professional Development in SEL

Design a timeline for PD in SEL that spans from August to June. Allow time for reflection to help build a sustainable program that reaches every stakeholder in every corner of the school building.

Before the start of the school year, make sure the following actions have been taken, using the information gathered from the principal (see Step 1 above), to build a solid foundation for PD programming.

1. Rally stakeholders and establish an SEL PD committee.
2. Review and revisit your state's SEL standards, the Call to Action (i.e. "Be the Solution") and the school's SEL vision.
3. Conduct a Pre-Survey (p. 150). Design a Common Language Document reflecting the marriage between school priorities, state SEL standards, and the school's SEL vision. Build consensus around teacher expectations (see Table 9.1) and adopt a rubric (p. 12).
4. Create a PD Calendar (see sample below). Send out a newsletter to school stakeholders introducing the SEL program and inviting all to attend the PD workshops. Keep an updated calendar, sign-in sheets, and incentivize participation.
5. Give teachers the time and resources to create SEL classrooms, including POP Charts and Call to Action messaging.

## Sample PD and Committee Meeting Calendar

August: SEL Committee Meeting – Establishing Baseline, Practices, and Expectations
September (start of school year): PD Session 1

**Table 9.1** SEL competencies for school stakeholders

| SEL competency | *"Looks like, sounds like, feels like"* | Strategies to build SEL competency |
|---|---|---|
| **Self-Awareness** | ◆ Self-esteem, positive self-talk, personal responsibility, and emotional awareness<br>◆ "I matter. I make a difference in students' lives. I set the tone for my classroom"<br>◆ "I OWN that my stress impacts my students. I am a powerful model of behavior"<br>◆ Body awareness and healthy lifestyle choices<br>◆ "It is my responsibility model self-care and healthy lifestyle choices for my students"<br>◆ Move from powerlessness to empowered | ◆ Brain Massage<br>◆ Yoga Sequence 1<br>◆ Yoga Sequence 2<br>◆ Write and Rip |
| **Self-Regulation** | ◆ Managing and expressing emotions appropriately<br>◆ "I reflect on my role in our school and the attitude I bring to situations"<br>◆ Adaptability, coping skills, and problem solving<br>◆ "I chose to find solutions and think creatively so that all needs are met"<br>◆ Move from impulsivity to positivity | ◆ Equal Breath<br>◆ Still Point<br>◆ Name It and Doodle It!<br>◆ Memory Minute |
| **Social Awareness** | ◆ Active listening skills, empathy, and community building<br>◆ "I know that I am a valued member of the school community and am aware that my positive energy, participation and collaboration impact those around me"<br>◆ Move from reactive and victimized to proactive and collaborative | ◆ Cooperation Circle<br>◆ Partner Mirroring<br>◆ Shoulder Share<br>◆ Boom Board! |
| **Balance between Self-Efficacy and Social Harmony** | ◆ Leadership, collaboration, teamwork<br>◆ "I appreciate the importance of teamwork and value my role in our school community. I chose to collaborate with others to Be the Solution, not the problem"<br>◆ Compassion with self and others<br>◆ "I realize that being compassionate with myself, my students and my colleagues is one of the most important things I do as an educator"<br>◆ Effectively balancing the needs of the SELF with the needs of the group (SOCIAL) | ◆ Goal Setting Postcard<br>◆ Compliment Partners<br>◆ Talking Stick<br>◆ Pass the Squeeze Circle and One-Word Check-In |

October: SEL Committee Meeting – Reviewing and Refining Practices and Expectations

November: PD Session 2

January: SEL Committee Meeting – Assessment of Skills Learned: Where are we and what do we need to improve?

February: PD Session 3

April: SEL Committee Meeting – On-going Implementation Assessment: How have we grown? What type of Service Learning Project would celebrate our growth?

May: PD Session 4

June: SEL Committee Meeting – On-going Implementation Assessment: Have we created a sustainable model?

## Step 4: Create an Emotionally and Physically Safe Professional Development Environment

Creating an emotionally and physically safe space is a critical element of a successful professional development session. Often, PD takes place in the auditorium or school cafeteria and very little is done to "set the stage" for sharing and reflection.

Included in the "Materials Needed" in the Facilitator's Guides in the next chapter are supplies to model the Agreements and the other communication tools found in teachers' SEL classrooms. Using these tools during professional development not only provides the teachers with a safe space to learn, it also experientially walks them through the same process as a learner that they are expected to facilitate as a practitioner.

The Agreements below are adapted from those developed by my dear friend Mario Rossero, Vice President of Education at the Kennedy Center. I find them exceptionally useful for framing any adult learning experience, as they "create a safe space for dialogue and critical conversation and aim to create equity of voice and ideas for sharing and growth."

The classroom sample Agreements are on page 42, but I have included an alternative version below specifically designed for PD. To practice cultural competency when introducing the Agreements, I like to invite the session participants to "propose any changes or amendments before we move forward." As many cultures have different conversational norms, this is a great way to build consensus around creating a safe space for all voices to be heard. Once the session has formally begun however, the Agreements are no longer open for adaptation.

Enforcing the Agreements is not easy. As I have already suggested, it is usually the participant that needs the Agreements the most that is the most resistant to their use. This resistance can take the form of outbursts, diatribes, or insubordination. It is important that the facilitator is prepared to match strength with strength. If a person is violating the safe space created by the Agreements, it is the facilitator's responsibility to honor the needs of the group and either help shift that person's behavior, or escort them out of the session. The needs of the individual cannot trump the needs of the group, even if her voice is the loudest and most impassioned one in the room.

## Professional Development Agreements

1. **Be fully present**
   - ◆ No food, phones, or anything that may distract you from our session.
2. **Speak your truth as you know it now**
   - ◆ Share only your story, not your friend's or something you heard.
3. **Accept and expect non-closure**
   - ◆ Sometimes questions and concerns will be left without answers or resolution.
4. **Remember the 24-hour rule**
   - ◆ There are only 24 hours to resolve conflicts from the session. No grudges: let it go.
5. **Watch your air time: 2 and 2**
   - ◆ 2 minutes max and 2 people speak before I share again. Original thoughts only: avoid piggybacking.
6. **Experience discomfort**
   - ◆ Expect to leave your comfort zone.
7. **Confidentiality**
   - ◆ After the session we may share work, but not personal stories that we heard today.
8. **\*Snaps\* and Table Taps**
   - ◆ Witness others' fabulousness and constructively find your voice when challenged or upset.

> ★ **Teacher Tip:** *Snaps* = participants snap three times in the air when they agree with the speaker. Table Taps = participants tap their fingers on a table if they witness someone breaking the Agreements or making a generalization, such as "Our parent community doesn't care about this school."

9. **Use our communication tools**
   - ◆ Pants on Fire!, Talking Stick, Boom Board!, *Snaps* and Table Taps.

10. **Honor our PD Experience**
   - ◆ Keep it compassionate, kind, equitable, safe, and inclusive.

As noted in number 9 above, I would also recommend Pants on Fire! (p. 107) and a Boom Board! (p. 105) for participants to share bright spots, challenges or factors that are keeping them from being fully present.

## Step 5: Implement Meaningful and Relevant Professional Development Content

My organization, Mindful Practices, has been providing high-quality professional development across the country since 2006 and I am proud to share with you our best practices. Agendas for three PD sessions, the Professional Development Facilitator's Guides, are outlined in Chapter 10.

If possible, implement the agendas in the time allotted and with the activities provided. The agendas are structured to build participant SEL competency from Self-Awareness to Self-Regulation to Social Awareness and on to find the balancing between Self-Efficacy and Social Harmony.

The sessions are experiential in nature and empower participants to read and respond proactively to their bodies' cues, to mirror the students' experience in the classroom. The union between the body and the mind is cultivated through four interconnected disciplines:

Vocalization: speaking, chanting, singing
Movement: gross/fine/locomotor, yoga, dance, fitness
Stillness: reflection, mindfulness, breathwork, meditation
Community-building: play, collaboration, communication

As with all professional development workshops, it is important that the pacing finds that delicate balance between modifying the content to meet the needs of the audience and maintaining the integrity of the delivery. Give the participants ample space to leave their comfort zones, be reflective, and take risks.

Include the Teacher Pre/Post Survey (p. 150) to help teachers monitor their own progress. This tool can easily be adapted for student use as well, if an informal progress monitoring tool is needed.

# 10

# Executing the Professional Development Facilitator's Guides

Included in this chapter are three Facilitator's Guides utilizing the activities and materials in this book. The sessions are designed to be experiential in nature, not merely a "sit and get," and average between 2 hours and 30 minutes to 3 hours in length.

If possible, it is recommended that each teacher have a copy of *Everyday SEL* in hand during the PD session. That way, they are able to turn to the corresponding page and make notes in real time after experientially participating in each activity. This process will help the teachers mentally bridge the gap between learner and facilitator and implement the activities with fidelity.

# Professional Development Facilitator's Guide: Session 1

## Beginning of the School Year

[School name]                                    [Date]

[Facilitator name and contact information]

**Topic:** Building Teacher Social-Emotional Learning Competency

"Relaxed teachers teach better. Relaxed students learn better." – Carla Tantillo Philibert

**Outcomes:** By attending this session, practitioners will:

1. Build their knowledge of Social-Emotional Learning (SEL).
2. Develop their SEL competency by experientially practicing strategies.
3. Build consensus around what SEL *looks like, sounds like, feels like* at [school name].
4. Develop the ability to model and encourage Self-Awareness and Self-Regulation in their classrooms, homes, and/or work with students.
5. Set goals for their implementation of SEL with consistency and fidelity.

**Estimated time:** 2.5–3 hours

**Audience:** __x___ teachers __x___ administrators __x___ support staff __x___ parents/community members ___x__ school stakeholders and faculty

**Materials needed:** Chart paper, markers, copies of *Everyday SEL*, index cards, small sticky notes, photocopies of rubric (p. 12), teacher pre/post-survey (p. 150) and copy of your state's SEL Standards, if applicable

**Room set-up:** Boom Board! (p. 105), Pants on Fire! (p. 107), POP Chart (p. 37), Thumbs-Up/Thumbs-Down Box (p. 35)

After each activity, the facilitator cues the participants to turn to the corresponding page in *Everyday SEL* to take notes in the margin. How can they amend the activity to work with their specific student population? What modifications should they make to allow for space/time constraints, to align with their academic content, and to meet the needs of their students with exceptionalities?

**SEL messaging by Principal [X]:** Why are you all here? Why is SEL a priority at our school? What do I expect to see over what timeline, and how will these expectations be mirrored in your evaluations? What is our Call to Action? Would a Call to Action, such as "Being In the Zone," "Being the Solution," or "Being Ready to Learn," work for us and our students? What does "Being In the Zone" look like for you, as an educator? – 20 minutes

**Facilitator begins**
*Administer Pre-Survey, if not already done.

1. Agreements for our PD session (p. 137) and using Agreements and Check for Understanding with your students (p. 42) – 20 minutes
2. The Mindful Practices approach (pp. 9, 10, 11, and 20), Getting Started (pp. 33 and 34) and your state's SEL standards, if applicable. What is our school's SEL goal? – 15 minutes
3. Brain Massage (p. 60) – 5 minutes
4. How to Use: Thumbs-Up/Thumbs-Down (pp. 38 and 39) – 5 minutes
5. How to Use: Boom Board! (p. 105) – 5 minutes
6. How to Use: Pants on Fire! (p. 107) – 5 minutes
7. Cooperation Circle (p. 86) into Pass the Clap (p. 93) – 20 minutes
8. Talking Stick (p. 110): If you bumped into a former student at the grocery store, would you rather she remembered the details of the academic content you delivered ("My two favorite elements were Strontium and Scandium because …") or that she had the skills to hold down a job, maintain positive relationships, and be a productive, compassionate citizen of the world? How does implementing SEL in our classrooms help us create life-long learners and achievers? How can we model "Being In the Zone," "Being the Solution," or "Being Ready to Learn" for our students daily? – 15 minutes
9. Crafting SEL Stories (p. 119) – 15 minutes
10. Yoga Sequence 1 (p. 61) – 10 minutes
11. Shoulder Share (p. 100): Review the SEL strategies you have learned so far today. Share how you can modify them to work with your students – 15 minutes

12. Ready to Learn Breath (p. 78) – 10 minutes
13. Debrief with Rubric (p. 12). Given what Principal [X] said at the beginning of our PD, what needs to be amended on the rubric to meet the specific needs of our school community? What are we already doing that is working? – 15 minutes
14. Goal Setting Postcard (p. 94) [Participants copy template onto an index card which is collected by facilitator and passed out at the start of the next PD session]

> "In the next two weeks I will implement the following activities
>
> with my students _____
>
> [list of activities] at this time _____ [list times]
>
> on these days _____ [list days]
>
> because _____ [list rationale for using SEL
>
> strategies]. My colleague _____ [write name
>
> of Thought Partner] will help support me, if I need additional
>
> resources and ideas. [Signed and dated by both participant and
>
> Thought Partner.] – 20 minutes

15. Pass the Squeeze Circle and One-Word Check-In (p. 91) – 5 minutes

# Professional Development Facilitator's Guide: Session 2

## Middle of the School Year

[School name]                                    [Date]

[Facilitator name and contact information]

**Topic:** Building Teacher Social-Emotional Learning Competency

"Teaching is subject to compassion." – Carla Tantillo Philibert

**Outcomes:** By attending this session, participants will:

1. Build their knowledge of Social-Emotional Learning (SEL).
2. Develop their SEL competency by experientially practicing strategies.
3. Build consensus around what SEL *looks like, sounds like, feels like* at [school name].
4. Model and encourage Self-Awareness, Self-Regulation, and Social Awareness in their classrooms, homes, and/or work with students.
5. Set goals for their implementation of SEL with consistency and fidelity.

**Estimated time:** 2.5–3 hours

**Audience:** __x__ teachers __x__ administrators __x__ support staff __x__ parents/community members ___x__ school stakeholders and faculty

**Materials needed:** Chart paper, markers, copies of *Everyday SEL*, index cards, small sticky notes, and photocopies of rubric

**Room set-up:** Boom Board!, Pants on Fire!, POP Chart, Thumbs-Up/ Thumbs-Down Box

After each activity, the facilitator cues the participants to turn to the corresponding page in *Everyday SEL* to take notes in the margin. How can they amend the activity to work with their specific student population? What modifications should they make to allow for space/time constraints, to align with their academic content and to meet the needs of their students with exceptionalities?

**Facilitator begins**

1. Review Agreements, Check for Understanding, Thumbs-Up/ Thumbs-Down, Boom Board! and Pants on Fire! – 15 minutes
2. Pass back Goal Setting Postcards. Debrief: Where am I with my goal? What are my successes? What are my challenges? Where do I need to ask for help? How can I support the school's SEL vision? – 15 minutes
3. Yoga Sequence 2 (p. 63) – 15 minutes
4. Pants on Fire! or Boom! Break – 10 minutes
5. Positive Paperchain (p. 104) – 10 minutes
6. Write and Rip (p. 70) – 10 minutes
7. Talking Stick: Many states have adopted Social-Emotional Learning standards without providing guidance on how teachers should be trained in SEL. Is that fair to teachers and students? Would standards for any other discipline, such as Music or Math, be adopted with the same assumption that all teachers are proficient in the delivery of that content? If you continue to reflect on your own SEL competency, where do you fall on the spectrum of Basic Needs ("fight or flight") to the Balance between Self-Efficacy and Social Harmony? (see Figure 1.2) – 20 minutes (principal stops in to facilitate, if possible)
8. Crafting SEL Stories – 15 minutes
9. Shoulder Share: Review the SEL strategies you have learned so far today. Share how you can modify them to work with our students during state testing time. – 15 minutes
10. Cotton Ball Breathing (p. 112) – 10 minutes
11. Select a volunteer to teach one of the SEL strategies learned today to the group (delivered as if teaching students) – 15 minutes
12. Debrief with Rubric: Does anything need to be amended on the rubric? Are we on track to meet the needs of our school community? – 10 minutes
13. Goal Setting Postcard [Collected by facilitator and passed out start of next PD session]

> In the next two weeks I will implement the following activities
>
> with my students _____
>
> [list of activities] at this time _____ [list times]
>
> on these days _____ [list days]

because _____ [list rationale for using SEL strategies]. My colleague _____ [write name of Thought Partner] will help support me, if I need additional resources and ideas. [Signed and dated by both participant and Thought Partner.] – 15 minutes

14. Pass the Squeeze Circle and One-Word Check-In – 5 minutes

## Professional Development Facilitator's Guide: Session 3

### End of the School Year

[School name]                                              [Date]

[Facilitator name and contact information]

**Topic:** Building Teacher Social-Emotional Learning Competency

"School is concurrently a personal and interpersonal enterprise for students. To be successful, students must artfully navigate both arenas at once." – Carla Tantillo Philibert

**Outcomes:** By attending this session, participants will:

1. Build their knowledge of Social-Emotional Learning (SEL).
2. Develop their SEL competency by experientially practicing strategies.
3. Build consensus around what SEL *looks like, sounds like, feels like* at [school name].
4. Model and encourage Self-Awareness, Self-Regulation, Social Awareness, Self-Efficacy, and Social Harmony in their classrooms, homes, and/or work with students.
5. Set goals for their implementation of SEL with consistency and fidelity.

**Estimated Time:** 2.5–3 hours

**Audience:** __x___ teachers __x___ administrators __x___ support staff __x___ parents/community members ___x__ school stakeholders and faculty

**Materials needed:** Chart paper, markers, copies of *Everyday SEL*, index cards, small sticky notes, photocopies of rubric and checklist

**Room set-up:** Boom Board!, Pants on Fire!, POP Chart, Thumbs-Up/ Thumbs-Down Box

After each activity, the facilitator cues the participants to turn to the corresponding page in *Everyday SEL* to take notes in the margin. How can they amend the activity to work with their specific student population?

What modifications should they make to allow for space/time constraints, to align with their academic content, and to meet the needs of their students with exceptionalities?

**Facilitator begins**

1. Review Agreements, Check for Understanding, Thumbs-Up/ Thumbs-Down, Boom Board! and Pants on Fire! – 10 minutes
2. Review school's vision for SEL this school year – 10 minutes
3. Pass back Goal Setting Postcards. Debrief: Where am I with my goal? What do I need to amend? Where do I need support to build a sustainable practice for next school year? – 10 minutes
4. Tap-In and Tap-Out (p. 89) – 10 minutes
5. Pants on Fire! or Boom! Break – 10 minutes
6. Partner Mirroring (p. 96) – 10 minutes
7. Talking Stick: To reinforce SEL's balance between Self-Efficacy and Social Harmony, the next step of the curriculum is to work collaboratively on a Service Learning Project (p. 116). What could a Service Learning Project look like at our school? How can we utilize our Call to Action to "Be the Solution" for our school community? – 20 minutes
8. Name It and Doodle It! (p. 81) – 10 minutes
9. Positive Paperchain – 5 minutes
10. Crafting SEL Stories – 15 minutes
11. Shoulder Share: Review the SEL strategies you have learned so far today. Share how you can modify them to work with our students so they have self-comforting strategies to use over the summer. – 10 minutes
12. Select a volunteer to teach one of the SEL strategies learned today to the group (delivered as if teaching students) – 10 minutes
13. Equal Breath (p. 80) – 5 minutes
14. Pants on Fire! or Boom! Break – 5 minutes
15. Compliment Partners (p. 98) – 10 minutes
16. Memory Minute (p. 84) – 5 minutes
17. Debrief with Rubric and checklist facilitated by Principal [X]: Now that it is the end of the school year, how have we met the needs of our school community? What are our successes? Have we fallen short? What is our game plan to build something sustainable for next year? How have you expanded your SEL competency and grown as a practitioner? – 10 minutes

18. Final Goal Setting Postcard [Collected by principal and mailed to participants over the summer]

Over the summer, I will reflect on how to revise and refine the following activities to use with my students _____ _____ [list of activities]. I will contact my colleague _____ [write name of Thought Partner] to help me brainstorm ways to build a sustainable SEL program for our school. If I need additional resources, I will email Principal [X] by _____ [date] with ideas and potential solutions. [Signed and dated by participant, Thought Partner and principal.] – 10 minutes

19. Pass the Squeeze and One-Word Check-In – 5 minutes

*Administer Teacher Post-Survey, if not already done.

# Appendix

# Teacher Pre/Post-Survey

## Please Circle the Number that Best Describes Your Response

Name:                                                    Date:

1. I understand how levels of energy (both my students' and mine) impact my classroom dynamic. I teach my students the life-long learning tools to relax, focus, and be present.

   1   Strongly disagree   2   Disagree   3   Agree   4   Strongly agree

2. I provide structure and effectively communicate procedures, protocols, and and reinforce boundaries with my students daily.

   1   Strongly disagree   2   Disagree   3   Agree   4   Strongly agree

3. I articulate clear, reasonable expectations for my students. I manage my classroom with consistency and fairness.

   1   Strongly disagree   2   Disagree   3   Agree   4   Strongly agree

4. I encourage my students to make decisions about their own learning. We set tangible, explicit, and meaningful goals about learning and behavior. My students are empowered to Be the Solution.

   1   Strongly disagree   2   Disagree   3   Agree   4   Strongly agree

5. I honor the Social-Emotional Learning needs of my students. I include daily mindfulness, breathing, and movement/yoga activities that help my students and me focus, concentrate, and be Ready to Learn.

   1   Strongly disagree   2   Disagree   3   Agree   4   Strongly agree

6. I create a classroom climate of "respect and rapport" in which my students feel both emotionally and physically safe.

   1   Strongly disagree   2   Disagree   3   Agree   4   Strongly agree

7. I make choices about food and drink for myself and my students that model a healthy lifestyle.

   1   Strongly disagree   2   Disagree   3   Agree   4   Strongly agree

8. I reflect on my practices as an educator and work hard to develop my Social-Emotional Learning competency. I know what behaviors from colleagues and students trigger me. I model the behaviors I want my students to exhibit. I OWN that I am a role model.

   1   Strongly disagree   2   Disagree   3   Agree   4   Strongly agree

# Be the Solution: Educator Questions from the Field

I began Mindful Practices in 2006 to empower teachers and students through Social-Emotional Learning, yoga, and wellness to create a more effective educational environment. In that time, my team and I have worked with a diverse cohort of schools with varying needs. Below is a sampling of questions that we often receive during program implementation. If your question is not answered here, please feel free to contact me directly to brainstorm solutions. It is important to me that practitioners have the tools and resources to implement SEL with fidelity.

**1. Problem:** I am the only one implementing SEL at my school. When I approached my principal with this concept she said, "Go ahead and try it; if it works in your room, then we can talk about implementing it next semester." How can I develop my own SEL competency along with my students, if there is **no SEL professional development** at my school?

**Solution:** First, share the professional development material (Chapters 9 and 10) with your principal. Ask her if you can teach a lesson during your next institute day. Then, offer a follow-up session before or after school for those teachers that are interested in learning more. This is great way to develop a small community of SEL innovators at your school site!

Additionally, along with practicing the SEL lessons you use with your students, you can also begin a reflective journal on these five areas of growth:

◆ Being explosive or emotionally reactive
◆ Advocating for personal or safe space
◆ Being compassionate with self and others
◆ Navigating difficult conversations
◆ Wrestling with perfectionism

Write in your reflective journal before school, after school, or during your preparatory period or your lunch. Any time you observe yourself or your students wrestling with or excelling on one of those five concepts, then cross-reference with the Teacher Survey (p. 150) to reflect on your findings.

**2. Problem:** I work with **students with exceptionalities**. While I love the Agreements, I fear that the guidelines are not "black and white" enough or are a little too abstract. Is there a different version of classroom rules I can use as an alternative?

**Solution:** Include shorter, more concise guidelines that you can act out. Stefanie, the lead instructor on my SEL team, uses this "rules" sequence. It is interactive to hold students' attention, and also simple and concise. (Act it out!)

> I need to see listening Eyes and Ears, scholars. Keep hands and feet to yourself. Let's quiet our mouths by zipping the lock and putting the key in your pocket. Listening Eyes – Let's all point to our eyes. If I'm talking and your eyes are on me, I know you can hear me and that you are trying your hardest to pay attention and follow directions. It also feels good to know that you can see me! Everyone give your arms a squeeze. Remember we keep our hands and feet to ourselves. This is especially important when we do bigger movements because we want to respect our neighbor's personal space. Quiet mouths – let's zip our lips, lock it, and put the key in our pocket [teacher mimes zipping, locking, and putting key in her pocket]. Remember that we have quiet mouths and big listening eyes and ears.

**3. Problem:** I only use exercise or yoga videos with my students, because my **classroom is so overcrowded**. I would love to use more authentic movement with students as part of their SEL time. How can I get them to stand without being on top of one another? And should I worry about parents' religious objections to yoga or mindfulness?

**Solution:** Each and every time you ask the students to stand, explicitly state, and model your expectations: "In Room 304 we respect our neighbors' personal space by keeping hands and feet to ourselves. We respect our community by refraining from jokes or comments. And we respect ourselves by listening to our bodies." As time goes by, this process will become quicker and quicker. Also, always preface that students will have 4 counts to gently pull their chair out, tuck it in, and stand behind their desks. If they are to return to a seated position, preface that students will have 4 counts to gently pull their chair out, sit down, and place hands on the desk. Personal space is a priority at all times.

Additionally, instead of turning to online resources, I encourage educators to practice yoga with their students, such as Yoga Sequence 1 (p. 61). Besides being an outlet for teachers themselves to get a bit of stress-relieving exercise, it also easily transitions to a student-led activity, fostering student leadership and cooperation. Once the class becomes accustomed to the procedures and protocols surrounding the activity, it is easy to have students create movement sequences to share with the class.

As for parents' potential religious objections to yoga or mindfulness, it is always best to err on the side of caution and send a note home to parents, explaining that yoga is the union of body and mind and that mindfulness is a practice that helps us be "in the now," or the present. Reassure them that no religion will be taught, but explain that the students will be moving through poses and that parents should let the school know if they or the student are uncomfortable so that alternative accommodations can be made.

**4. Problem:** I love using movement to energize my class, but **I teach students with limited physical mobility.** Is there a class song or cheer I can use instead that is accessible for all?

**Solution:** Try this Class Song, sung to the tune of "The Rubber Ducky Song"

> *Room 204*
> *You're the one*
> *You make school lots of fun*
> *Room 204 I'm awfully found of YOU*
> *Boo boo be do!*
> *Room 204*
> *You're full of heart*
> *You try your best and you're really smart*
> *Room 204 you're a really great class it's true*
> *boo boo be do!*
> *[Use during transitions. Repeat.]*

**5. Problem:** I am a principal and I want to **start our day with a positive** breathing activity to build our school climate and culture. Any ideas?

**Solution:** Say the following as part of the announcements every morning.

> We try our best.
> We are responsible for our own behavior.
> We are self-aware and know how to self-soothe and calm down.
> We are important members of our school community.
> We are the Solution. We are In the Zone and Ready to Learn!

Then, roll into "We are – We are – the Solution (clap clap) – the Solution (clap clap)! We are – We are – the Solution (clap clap)! The Solution (clap clap)!"

(Sung to the tune of "We Will Rock You")

Depending on teachers' comfort levels, you can ask them to have students clap or pound on desks or move in and out of their favorite yoga pose as a great way to let go of excess energy.

To bring students back to a calm, focused place, conclude with 10 Ready to Learn Breaths (p. 78).

**6. Problem:** Many of my students **live in poverty** and have a difficult time with the concepts of **personal space and safe touch.** Is there a way I can pre-teach the concepts before introducing movement into my classroom?

**Solution:** Read the scripts below. Highlight the parts that resonate for you and your students. After you have established the Agreements (p. 42), use these pieces as a jumping off point for a safe and open class discussion. Prior to the discussion, review your legal obligations as a Mandated Reporter. Additionally, remind the students that they can put any thoughts, questions or concerns into the Thumbs-Up/Thumbs-Down Box that they don't want to share with the entire class.

## Personal Space

Asking for personal space is creating a respectful boundary for yourself and those around you. Picture yourself in a situation when your physical or emotional space is not being respected. Maybe you are around someone who is getting too close and it doesn't feel right or it makes you feel weird in your body. Maybe someone is expressing their anger in a way that makes you feel unsafe. Or, maybe you are in a challenging situation where you feel like your voice is not being heard. Often, when we are in one of these situations, we don't say anything because we don't want to hurt the other person's feelings or cannot find our words. But, we must always remember that someone else's comfort is NEVER more important than our safety. Even someone that is close to us – a cousin, a friend, an aunt or uncle, a coach, a parent – may need help remembering that everyone deserves their own physical and emotional safe space. Take a breath and picture yourself asking for safe space. Find your voice. Use your words. Maybe you say, "Please stop. What you are doing doesn't make me feel safe." Or, "Please stop. I would like you take three steps back and honor my personal space." Take another breath and picture the other person hearing your request. He may be able to honor your request nicely, he may be confused and need an explanation or he may get upset and be offended. However he responds, it doesn't mean that you were wrong to request personal space. It just means he was not ready to hear you. That is OK. You may need to firmly remind him again. Remember, EVERYONE has a right to her own physical and emotional safe space.

## Safe Touch

[Teacher models, students follow along.]
*Safe touch is ...* [Students repeat]
*Head to Shoulders.* [Teacher motions towards head, moves down to shoulders. Students repeat words and mirror motioning action.]
*Shoulders to Hands.* [Teacher motions towards shoulders, moves down to hands. Students repeat words and mirror actions.]
*Knees to Feet.* [Teacher motions towards knees, moves down to feet. Students repeat words and mirror actions.]
Repeat sequence
[Teacher closes with a question-and-answer session with students reinforcing What Is and What Is Not safe touch. Teacher reinforces that the rules of safe touch apply at both school and home and that a student should share with him/her if someone in their lives is not honoring the rules of safe touch and is violating their personal space.]

**7. Problem:** I am a school administrator and I need more ideas on **including Be the Solution**, our Call to Action, across disciplines. I am having a hard time getting buy-in from our auxiliary staff.

**Solution:** Invite your **school community** to get involved in the school's daily routines, such as morning announcements. "School stakeholders, let's start our day the Be the Solution Way!"

School stakeholders are the faces that shape your students' educational experience. This includes classroom teachers, bus drivers, specials teachers, custodians, cafeteria staff, social workers, recess staff, parents, and community members (see p. 20).

"Our students at [x] School are everyone's responsibility. Each role has value." No one in the school is viewed as a babysitter or an "invisible" cog in the system. Each person is valued and each person is expected to model Be the Solution behavior and messaging for the students.

Stakeholders are taken from class to class and introduced to students at the beginning of the year. When possible, money is set aside to compensate stakeholders for attending, and participating in, SEL PD trainings, holiday assemblies, faulty meetings, etc., as, being that they may be part-time employees, they may need to take time off work at another job to attend. The students see that everyone is a stakeholder in their school community.

Below are some examples of ways to get school stakeholders involved in the morning announcements. A fun and visible way to build community every morning.

### Empower Student or Recess Facilitator

Good Morning Calogero School students! Given that it is only 15 degrees outside today, outdoor recess will be cancelled. So, let's Be the Solution and find a way to prioritize physical movement into today's schedule. It is important that both our minds and bodies are Ready to Learn. I have asked one of Ms. Inez's Recess Captains to lead us through some movement and yoga during our morning announcements. When your teacher gives you the signal, please stand up, push in your chairs, and stand behind your desks. I will now turn the microphone over to Ms. Inez and her Recess Captain, Connor Phillips from Room 404, to lead us through some movement. Please remember, as always, to respect your neighbor's personal space and your body's physical needs. It is not important to do every move perfectly; the most important thing is to try your best.

Ms. Inez introduces her Recess Captain who gets on the microphone and leads the school through a series of physical movements appropriate for the classroom. A sample series may include:

Jogging in Place (count of 10)
Mountain Pose (5 breaths)
Tree Pose (right leg, 5 breaths)
Tree Pose (left leg, 5 breaths)

Jogging in Place (count of 10)
Mountain Pose (5 breaths)
Seated Arm Stretch (10 breaths)
Close: Ready to Learn Breath (p. 78)

If possible, it is great to alert the teachers prior to the start of the school day, so they know that the announcements will be a few minutes longer than usual. Also, selecting a few students to be "on call" for this activity is great. They are able to prepare their routines ahead of time, and even practice them at home for their families.

## Recruit Your Media Specialist or Music Teacher to Lend a Hand

The Media Specialist can read a short but appropriately themed SEL Story, such as Scholastic's *Love Monster*, by Rachel Bright, over the loud speaker. Every time she reads the word "Cute" the students jog in place (for five breaths) and every time she reads the word "Monster" the students find Starfish Pose (for five breaths).

For a more advanced approach, the Music teacher can play multiple types of instruments. Each time the teacher plays a percussive instrument, the students Freestyle Dance (for five breaths), each time he plays a wind instrument the students hold Horse pose (for five breaths), each time he plays a string instrument the students do Jumping Jacks (for five breaths), and each time he plays an electronic instrument the students hold Starfish Pose (for five breaths).

To keep consistency, each of these experiences should end with a Ready to Learn Breath, rolling into a one-word check-in facilitated by the classroom teacher.

## Recruit Your PE Teacher

A 60-second "Be Solution Meditation" written by school stakeholder Awan Blackhawk, the PE teacher, is read to the whole school over the loud speaker. This is a great opportunity for the teacher to reinforce the Be the Solution behavior that he would like to see in his PE room, such as proper use of equipment or respecting personal space. The principal warmly introduces him, "I am happy to welcome Mr. Blackhawk, our PE teacher, to share his Be the Solution Minute with us this morning." Mr. Blackhawk reads the meditation, and then the principal cues the beginning and ending of activity by announcing, "Your 60 seconds of silence begins/ends now." The principal then thanks "Mr. Blackhawk, for sharing his Be the Solution Minute with Dorothy Adam Elementary School this morning. I agree it is important that we all remember to respect our PE equipment. That equipment was purchased for us all to share and so we must handle it carefully and with respect."

To bring the activity back to the classroom once the announcement has concluded, the classroom teacher gets a one-word check-in from her students. How are they feeling? Are they ready to start the day? (This is another great opportunity for teachers to notice if student energy has shifted since their POP Chart Check-In at the start of the day.)

**8. Problem:** I love using a Call to Action to get students motivated! Can I have a few more examples of **how it can help transitions**, when time is tight?

**Solution:** Room 314 is in working in cooperative groups when the fire alarm goes off. It is time for a fire drill! When the students return to their classroom, they are already late for lunch. Ms. Jenkins, the teacher, needs the room cleaned up before lunch because the students will be taking a math test when they come back.

Ms. Jenkins announces, "OK Room 314, it is time to **Be the Solution!**" She goes to the board and quickly writes the following:

Be the Solution: Cleaning up after group work
Activity: Preparing our room for our math test!
Time start: 11:04
Time stop: 11:06

Alternatively, a teacher senses that her classroom is really nervous before a test. She wants them to practice a quick activity to get centered and focused.

OK, Room 410, our class needs to get **In the Zone** and focus before our big test. I am looking for a student respecting the Agreements, who can go to the POP Chart and choose an activity to help us out. Given that we are not taking this test in groups and we need to stay seated, let's choose an activity from the SELF side of the POP Chart. Lee Sun Yew, thank you for sitting quietly and actively listening. Will you pick an activity that can help our class get In the Zone and focus?

Once the activity has been chosen, the teacher writes the time and activity on the board.

Be In the Zone: Focus for our test
Activity: Memory Minute
Time start: 1:02
Time stop: 1:03
Lee Sun Yew facilitates the activity as the teacher acts as timer.

**9. Problem:** I need a few more examples of how I can use **both structured and unstructured movement** with my students.

**Solution:** Practicing movement prior to group work or a test is a great way to help the class release excess energy that can often make being present and focused challenging for your more frenetic **students**. For **a structured approach**, select a student who is exhibiting Be the Solution behavior to lead the your students through a sequence of physical movements appropriate for the classroom. You can write a sequence on the board, such as:

10 Jumping Jacks
Tree Pose (5 breaths)
10 Jumping Jacks
Tree Pose (5 breaths)
Seated Arm Stretch (10 breaths)

If time permits, have that student choose a peer to lead the class through a mindfulness or relaxation activity like Ready to Learn Breath or select a favorite activity from the POP Chart to close the session.

For **a less structured approach** or when working with a reluctant group, put on music and declare "Free Dance" for the next 90 seconds. Students can move in whatever way they feel comfortable (fast or slow, subtle, or grand), as long as they are respecting their neighbor's personal space and using moves appropriate for school (i.e. no fighting gestures, miming sexual positions, or fake firing of weapons). When you feel the students' energy beginning to settle down, shift to calmer music and ask the students to slowly find their seats. Once they are seated, close the session with a centering activity like Memory Minute (p. 84).

**10. Problem:** The SEL competencies are too vague for my students. How can I make SEL more explicit and concrete in my classroom?

**Solution:** Create a chart of what behaviors "do" and "don't" look, sound and feel like for your classroom and post it next to your POP Chart. Begin simply, by identifying behaviors that you most want your students to focus on, such as active listening. There will most likely be some redundancy in your messaging, but that is OK. The most important thing is to use culturally relevant examples and explicit observable behaviors, so that students can develop their competency and voice around the SEL concepts.

**Table A.1** Explicit Teaching: Active listening

| Active listening<br>looks like<br>sounds like<br>feels like | Active listening **does not**<br>look like<br>sound like<br>feel like |
| --- | --- |
| ◆ using our Talking Stick<br>◆ respecting the Agreements<br>◆ finding our voices<br>◆ being present<br>◆ using Be the Solution behavior by sitting up tall with eyes and bodies toward the speaker<br>◆ respecting others' feelings, emotions, and opinions so all voices can be heard<br>◆ using our communication tools, like Boom Board!, Pants on Fire! or the Thumbs-Up/Thumbs-Down Box<br>◆ being culturally sensitive and respectful<br>◆ honoring our physically and emotionally safe classroom | ◆ eye rolling, grunting, or making comments under our breath<br>◆ breaking the Agreements<br>◆ focusing our attention on distractions, like phones, iPads, or food<br>◆ laughing at others' feelings, emotions, and opinions<br>◆ making negative comments like "that's stupid" or "what a dumb idea!"<br>◆ dominating the group with your voice<br>◆ speaking negatively or making assumptions about others' races or cultures<br>◆ dishonoring our physically and emotionally safe space by saying "Shut up," starting a fight or violating others' personal space |

# References and Further Reading

Acedo, C., Opertti, R., Brady, J., and Duncombe, L. Interregional and Regional Perspectives on Inclusive Education: Follow-up of the 48th Session of the International Conference on Education. Paris: United Nations Educational, Scientific and Cultural Organization, 2011.

Brown, Brene. *The Gifts of Imperfection: Let Go of Who You Think You're Supposed to Be and Embrace Who You Are*. Center City, MI: Hazelden, 2010.

Cole, J., and Calmenson, S. *The Eentsy, Weentsy Spider*. New York: Mulberry Books, 1991.

Collaborative for Academic, Social, and Emotional Learning (CASEL). CASEL.org.

Cook-Cottone, C. P. *Mindfulness and Yoga for Self-Regulation: A Primer for Mental Health Professionals*. New York: Springer, 2015.

Danielson, C., and Chicago Public Schools (CPS). *CPS Framework for Teaching Companion Guide: Version 1.0*. Chicago: CPS, 2011.

Farhi, Donna. *The Breathing Book: Good Health and Vitality through Essential Breath Work*. New York: Henry Holt, 1996.

Fullan, Michael. *Change Leader: Learning to do What Matters Most*. San Francisco: Jossey-Bass, 2011.

Goleman, D., and Senge, P. *The Triple Focus: A New Approach to Education*. Florence, MA: More Than Sound, 2014.

Hackney, Peggy. *Making Connections: Total Body Integration Through Bartenieff Fundamentals*. New York: Routledge, 2002.

Hargreaves, A., and Fullan, M. *Professional Capital: Transforming Teaching in Every School*. New York: Teachers College Press, 2012.

Harrison, L. J., Manocha, R., and Rubia, K. Sahaja Yoga Meditation as a Family Treatment for Children with Attention Deficit–Hyperactivity Disorder. *Clinical Child Psychology and Psychiatry*, 9 (2004): 479–497.

Hattie, J. *Visible Learning: A Synthesis of Over 800 Meta-Analyses Relating to Achievement*. New York: Routledge, 2009.

Illinois State Board of Education (ISBE). Social-Emotional Learning Standards. ISBE.state.il.us., n.d.

Illinois State Board of Education. Special Education and Support Services: Service Learning Guide. ISBE.state.il.us, 2006.

Illinois State Board of Education. Illinois Early Learning and Development Standards. ISBE.state.il.us, 2013.

Jha, A. P., Krompinger, J., and Baime, M. J. Mindfulness Training Modifies Subsystems of Attention. *Journal of Cognitive Affective and Behavioral Neuroscience*, 7 (2007): 109–119.

Jones, D. Healthy and Smart: Using Wellness to Boost Performance. *Principal Leadership*, 8/4 (2007): 32–36. ERIC (EJ780560).

Jones, S., Bouffard, S., and Weissbourd, R. Educators' Social and Emotional Skills Vital to Learning. *Kappan Magazine*, 94/8 (2013): 62–65.

Kabat-Zinn, J. *Full Catastrophe Living: Using the Wisdom of Your Body and Mind to Face Stress, Pain and Illness.* New York: Dell, 1990.

Kripalu Center for Yoga and Health. *Kripalu Yoga in the Schools Curriculum.* Stockbridge, MA: Kripalu, 2015.

Lemov, Doug. *Teach Like a Champion: 49 Techniques that Put Students on the Path to College.* San Francisco: Jossey-Bass, 2010.

Linden, W. Practicing of Meditation by School Children and their Levels of Field Dependence-Independence, Test Anxiety and Reading Achievement. *Journal of Consulting and Clinical Psychology*, 41 (1973): 139–143.

McKinley, Johnnie. *Raising Black Students' Achievement through Culturally Responsive Teaching.* Alexandria, VA: Association for Supervision and Curriculum Development, 2010.

Purcell, M., and Murphy, J. *Mindfulness for Teen Anger.* Oakland, CA: New Harbinger Publications, 2014.

Rubin, Gretchen. *The Happiness Project.* New York: HarperCollins, 2011.

Senge, P., Cambron-McCabe, N., Lucas, T., Smith, B., Dutton, J., and Kleiner, A. *Schools that Learn: A Fifth Discipline Fieldbook for Educators, Parents, and Everyone Who Cares About Education.* New York: Crown Business, 2012.

Siegel, R. *The Science of Mindfulness: A Research-Based Path to Well-Being.* The Great Courses, 2014 (audio).

Spolin, Viola. *Theatre Games for the Classroom: A Teacher's Handbook.* Chicago: Northwestern University Press, 1986.

Stueck, M., and Gloeckner, N. Yoga for Children in the Mirror of the Science: Working Spectrum and Practice Fields of the Training of Relaxation with Elements of Yoga for Children. *Early Child Development and Care*, 175/4 (2005): 371–377.

Tantillo, C., and Crowley, E. *Cooling Down Your Classroom: Using Yoga, Relaxation and Breathing Strategies to Help Students Learn to Keep Their Cool.* Chicago: Mindful Practices, 2012.

Wessler, Stephen, and Preble, William. *The Respectful School: How Educators and Students Can Conquer Hate and Harassment*. Alexandria, VA: Association for Supervision and Curriculum Development, 2003.

Willard, C. *Mindfulness for Teen Anxiety*. Oakland, CA: Instant Help Publications, 2014.

Wong, Harry K., and Rosemary T. Wong. *The First Days of School: How to Be an Effective Teacher*. Mountain View, CA: Harry K. Wong Publications, 2009.